MUSEUM MONOGRAPHS

ENMERKAR AND THE LORD OF ARATTA
A SUMERIAN EPIC TALE OF IRAQ AND IRAN

SAMUEL NOAH KRAMER

WIPF & STOCK · Eugene, Oregon

Wipf and Stock Publishers
199 W 8th Ave, Suite 3
Eugene, OR 97401

Enmerkar and the Lord of Aratta
A Sumerian Epic Tale of Iraq and Iran
By Kramer, Samuel Noah
Softcover ISBN-13: 978-1-6667-5072-0
Hardcover ISBN-13: 978-1-6667-5073-7
eBook ISBN-13: 978-1-6667-5074-4
Publication date 6/15/2022
Previously published by The University Museum, 1952

This edition is a scanned facsimile of the original edition published in 1952.

ENMERKAR AND THE LORD OF ARATTA:

A SUMERIAN EPIC TALE OF IRAQ AND IRAN

by

Samuel Noah Kramer

CONTENTS

ACKNOWLEDGMENT

The author wishes to express his heartfelt thanks to the Directorate of Antiquities of the Turkish Republic. Orientalists the world over owe a profound debt of gratitude to the Turkish Directorate of Antiquities for its generous coöperation in helping to make available its invaluable collection of Sumerian literary tablets for study and publication.

INTRODUCTION

ONE OF the more significant cultural achievements of the ancient Sumerians was the creation and development of epic poetry, a literary genre hitherto associated primarily with such Indo-European peoples as the Greeks, Hindus, and Teutons. It consists of heroic narrative tales composed in a highly distinctive poetic form which celebrate the deeds and exploits of those kings and princes whose experiences lent themselves to sympathetic and imaginative treatment by the bards and minstrels of their day. At present it is possible to identify nine such Sumerian epic tales (see for the present "Heroes of Sumer: A New Heroic Age in World History and Literature," *Proceedings* of the American Philosophical Society, vol. 90, pp. 120-130). They revolve about the heroes Enmerkar, Lugalbanda, and Gilgamesh, all of whom lived in the Sumerian "Heroic Age," a period which may perhaps be dated to the first century of the third millennium B.C. The poem published in this monograph is the largest of the Sumerian epic tales as yet discovered. It portrays primarily the bitter rivalry between Enmerkar, the ruler of the city-state of Erech in southern Mesopotamia, and an unnamed "lord" of Aratta, a city-state to be sought somewhere in southern Iran, perhaps in modern Laristan. In the course of the narrative the poet introduces a considerable number of descriptive details which are highly significant for the history and culture of the ancient Near East, particularly for the Sumero-Iranian culture complex as it shaped up some five thousand years ago. In particular, our epic tale (together with two other epic tales involving Enmerkar, tentatively entitled "Enmerkar and Sukushsiranna" and "Lugalbanda and Enmerkar," which will be edited and translated in the near future) provides us with the first written records relating to an early proto-Iranian civilization which had hitherto been known from material archaeological finds only. First, however, a brief sketch of the contents of our epic tale, based on the tentative translation presented for the first time in this monograph.

The poem begins with a preamble (lines 1-32), the text of which is poorly preserved; it seems to sing the greatness of Erech and Kullab (a district within Erech or in its immediate neighborhood) from the very beginning of time, and its closing lines stress its superiority over Aratta as a result of the goddess Inanna's preference. The real action then begins with the words "once upon a time." Once upon a time, our poet continues, Enmerkar, son of the sun-god Utu, having determined to make a vassal state of Aratta, uttered a plea before his sister, the goddess Inanna, that the people of Aratta bring gold, silver, lapis lazuli, and precious stones, and build for him various shrines and temples, particularly the Apsû-temple in Eridu (lines 33-64). Inanna heeds his plea. She advises him to seek out a suitable herald to cross the imposing mountains of Anshan, which separate Erech from Aratta, and assures him that the people of Aratta will submit to him and carry out the building operations which he desires (lines 65-104). Enmerkar selects his herald and sends him to Aratta with a message threatening to destroy and make desolate his city unless he and his people bring down silver and gold and build and decorate for him Enki's temple. To further impress the lord of Aratta, Enmerkar instructs his herald to repeat to him the "spell of Enki" which relates how the god Enki had put an end to man's "golden age" under Enlil's universal sway over the earth and its inhabitants (lines 105-160).

The herald, after a journey which involves the crossing of seven mountains, arrives at Aratta, duly repeats his master's words to its lord, and asks for his answer (lines 161-218). The latter, however, refuses to yield to Enmerkar, since he claims to be Inanna's protégé who had brought him to Aratta as its ruler (lines 219-227). Whereupon the herald informs him that be that as it may, Inanna, who had now been made "Queen of Eanna" in Erech, had promised Enmerkar that Aratta would submit to him (lines 228-236). The lord of Aratta is at first stunned by this news, but he recovers and finds an answer for the herald to take back to his king. In it he admonishes Enmerkar for resorting to arms; he himself prefers the "contest" that is, perhaps, a fight between two selected champions. But if Enmerkar will send Aratta large quantities of grain, he is ready to submit to him, since Inanna has become Aratta's enemy (lines 237-294). The herald returns to Erech "on the double" and delivers the message to Enmerkar in the courtyard of the assembly hall (lines 295-308).

Before making his next move Enmerkar performs several acts which seem to be ritualistic in character, and takes counsel with Nidaba, the Sumerian goddess of wisdom. He then has his beasts of burden loaded with grain and sends them to Aratta accompanied by the herald who is to deliver to its lord a message eulogizing Enmerkar's scepter and commanding him to bring Enmerkar carnelian and lapis lazuli (lines 309-347). The herald arrives with the cargo of grain which he heaps up in the courtyard of Aratta, and its delighted people are ready to present Enmerkar with the desired carnelian (nothing seems to be said of the lapis lazuli) and to have the "elders" build his "pure house" for him (lines 348-377). But when the herald repeats Enmerkar's message, the crestfallen and practically hysterical lord of Aratta, after eulogizing his own scepter, insists in words identical with those of Enmerkar that the latter bring him carnelian and lapis lazuli (lines 378-412).

Upon the herald's return to Erech, Enmerkar now seems to consult the omens, in particular one involving a reed *šusima*, which he brings forth from "light to shade" and from "shade to light," until he finally cuts it down "after five years, after ten years had passed." He then sends forth the herald once again to Aratta, this time merely placing the scepter in his hand and without any accompanying message (lines 413-435). The sight of the scepter seems to arouse terror in the lord of Aratta. He turns to his *šatammu*, and after speaking bitterly of the plight of his city as a result of Inanna's displeasure, he seems ready to yield to Enmerkar. Nevertheless, he once again issues a challenge to Enmerkar demanding that the latter select one of his fighting-men as his representative to engage in single combat with one of his own fighting-men as his (the lord of Aratta's) representative, and thus "the strong(er) will become known." Moreover, he words the challenge in riddle-like terms, asking that the selected retainer be neither black nor white, neither brown, yellow, nor dappled—all of which seems to make little sense when speaking of a man (lines 436-462).

Upon the herald's arrival at Erech with this new challenge, Enmerkar bids him return to Aratta with a threefold message. First, he (Enmerkar) accepts the lord of Aratta's challenge and is prepared to send one of his retainers to fight his Aratta counterpart to a decision. Moreover, he seems to resolve the lord of Aratta's riddle-like phrases by substituting the word "garment" for "fighting-man," that is, presumably the color referred to garments which the combatants wore rather than to their bodies. Secondly, Enmerkar demanded that the lord of Aratta heap up gold, silver, and precious stones for the goddess Inanna in Erech. In the third part of the message Enmerkar once again threatens Aratta with total destruction unless its lord and people bring "stones of the mountain," and build and decorate for him the Eridu shrine (lines 463-497).

There follows a remarkable passage, which, if correctly interpreted, informs us that Enmerkar, the lord of Kullab, was, in the opinion of the poet, the first to write on clay tablets; he did so because for some reason--perhaps because of its length--the herald seemed "heavy of mouth," and unable to repeat the message (lines 498-507). The herald delivers the inscribed tablet to the lord of Aratta and awaits his answer (lines 508-536). But help now seems to come to the lord of Aratta from an unexpected source. The Sumerian god of rain and storm, Ishkur, brings to Aratta wild growing wheat and beans(?) and heaps them up before the lord of Aratta. At the sight of the wheat the latter takes courage and regains his confidence; he informs Enmerkar's herald that Inanna had by no means abandoned Aratta and her house and bed in it (lines 537-564).

From here on the text becomes fragmentary and the context is difficult to follow. The translation assumes that lines 565-601 consist of straight narrative. The first part of the passage (lines 565-577) seems to describe the destruction of Aratta by a raging flood, and its revival by Inanna. Lines 578-588 seem to tell of the arrival of (perhaps) Enmerkar's "champion," dressed in helmet and lion-skins; also of someone perfecting the rites and feasts, perhaps for the god Dumuzi. The remainder of the passage (lines 589-600, as far as it is at all intelligible, describes the arrival of an unnamed "old woman" who seems to bring out (either for Dumuzi or for the "champion") a maid with painted eyes and white garments. Line 601 seems to introduce a speech, but the identity of the individuals involved is uncertain; its contents (lines 602-615) are too fragmentary for an intelligent guess. The remainder of the poem (lines 616-637) is altogether obscure except for the reasonably certain statement that the people of Aratta did bring gold, silver, and lapis lazuli to Erech and heaped them up in the courtyard of Eanna for Inanna.

So much for the brief sketch of the contents of the poem. As mentioned above our epic tale is particularly significant for the light it sheds on the otherwise practically unknown ancient Iranian city-state of Aratta; it provides us with a number of revealing details relating to Aratta's geography, political organization, economy, and religion, all of which are almost entirely new. The troublesome and disturbing problem to bear constantly in mind, of course, is just how many of these details are historically trustworthy. For in the first place, the tablets on which the poem is inscribed date, rough-ly speaking, from about 1700 B.C.; its major protagonist, the hero Enmerkar, on the other hand, proba-bly lived more than a millennium earlier, roughly about 3000 B.C. (see *American Journal of Ar-chaeology*, vol. 52, pp. 163-164). To be sure, the extant tablets on which the poem is inscribed may be copies of older and as yet unexcavated texts. But the oldest could not be earlier than the second half of the third millennium B.C., which would still date them centuries later than the period with which our epic tale is concerned. However, there is little doubt that, as in the case of the Indo-European epics, the written Sumerian tales are highly modified redactions of oral lays which were first composed by court minstrels and bards during the lifetime of the kings and heroes whose deeds and adventures they celebrate. It is therefore not unjustifiable to conclude that as in the case of the Iliad, for example, there is at least a core of historic truth in the events which our tale narrates and in the socio-political background which it depicts.

Turning now to Aratta's geographic location, our poem indicates that it is situated in a mountainous region which is separated from Erech, in southern Mesopotamia, by a series of mountain ranges (lines 73, 74, 108, 109, 171, etc., etc.) which made communication between them difficult and hazardous. Moreover, Aratta is related in some way to the land Anshan, generally located immediately to the south of Elam (lines 75, 76, 108, 109, etc.). The statement in our poem is obscure, but fortunately the still unedited epic tale "Lugalbanda and Enmerkar" supplements it significantly. There it is stated that in order to get to Aratta from Erech, the hero Lugalbanda had to cross seven mountains from the "side" of Anshan to the "head" of Anshan, that is, presumably from its upper end to its lower end (see *Bulletin of the American Schools of Oriental Research*, no. 96, p. 26). We may there-fore conclude that Aratta was situated somewhere below Anshan in southwestern Iran, perhaps in modern Laristan.

As for Aratta's political organization, we note its head and ruler was the *en*, "lord," or perhaps "high-priest" (the title "king" seems to be unknown in Aratta, and it is noteworthy that Enmerkar, too, was known primarily by the title *en*, although he is described as *lugal*, "king," several times in our poem (see lines 306, 311, 316, etc.). There were also such officials as "knight" (line 364), *išakku* (line 440), *šatammu* (line 444), "supervisors" (line 556). Mentioned, too, are "the elders" (line 374), and an assembly met in Aratta according to the companion epic tale "Enmerkar and Ensukushsiranna" (line 127 of the still unedited and tentative reconstruction of the text), just as it did in Erech (see *American Journal of Archaeology*, vol. 53, pp. 6 ff.).

Aratta's economic wealth, as might have been surmised from its geographic situation, consisted primarily of gold, silver, and all kinds of stone; moreover, it was noted for its skilled metal and stone workers, its masons and sculptors. It was for this reason, no doubt, that the rulers of Erech, a region destitute of stones and metals, were eager to add Aratta to their domain. On the other hand, Aratta was evidently not rich in grain, of which Erech had a surplus; hence, perhaps, a readiness on the part of her people to yield to Erech in spite of the wishes of their ruler.

Of no little interest, finally, are the passages in our tale which reveal the poet's tradition concern-ing the religion of Aratta. According to him, its people worship the Sumerian pantheon, and the deities whose cults were particularly popular were Dumuzi (see lines 96-101, 564 ff.) and Inanna (see lines 221-226, 286-291, 558 ff.), although the latter is the patron-deity of Erech. The god Enki, on the other hand, who is a high favorite of Enmerkar (see lines 54-58, 128 ff.), seems to be inimical to Aratta (see line 119). All in all, therefore, if our poet's tradition is at all authentic, we may conclude that at the end of the fourth and the beginning of the third millennium B.C., the city-state of Aratta, though situated in a mountainous region of Iran far from Sumer, was under Sumerian cultural and politi-cal domination. Indeed it is not impossible that its ruling caste consisted of Sumerians, for while the lord of Aratta remains unnamed throughout our poem, he bears the good Sumerian name Ensukushsiranna in the companion epic tale "Enmerkar and Ensukushsiranna."

The text of our poem is reconstructed from twenty tablets and fragments, of which the most important by far is the twelve-column tablet Ni 9601, copied in the Museum of the Ancient Orient during my stay in Istanbul in the fall of 1946, to which the University Museum fragment UM 29-13-194 is to be joined (for details, see *Bulletin of the American Schools of Oriental Research*, no. 104, pp. 10 ff.). All the pieces date from the early post-Sumerian period, that is, from the first half of the second millennium B.C., and were excavated by the first University of Pennsylvania expedition to Nippur toward the end of the nineteenth century; they are now located in the Museum of the Ancient Orient in Istanbul and in the University Museum of the University of Pennsylvania in Philadelphia. In detail, they are as fol-lows: Ni 9601+UM 29-13-194=A (plates I-XIII, XVII-XIX); N 4130=B (plate XIX); UM 29-16-422=C (plates XIV, XX); N 6277=D (plate XXI); *SEM* 14= E (plates XXII, XXIII); *SRT* 34= F; *PBS* XIII 8=G (plate XXIV); Ni 4529= H (plate XV); N 3236=I (plate XXIV); *SEM* 16= J (plates XXV, XXVI); Ni 4361+ 4440=K (plate XVI); Ni 9733=L (plate XIII); *SEM* 15= M; Ni 9700=N (plate XIII); N 3632=O (plate XXVIII); *HGT* 8= P (plate XXVII); BE XXXI 44= Q; N 3623=R (plate XXVII); *HAV* 9=S; CBS 2291= T (plate XXVIII).

Line by line the reconstruction of the text is as follows: 1-end= A; 11-21=B obv. i; 25-37= C obv. i; 31(?)-38= D obv; 55-86= E obv. i; 66-72= B obv. ii; 71-84= F obv. ii; 75-94= C obv. ii; 104-119= G obv. ii, rev. iii; 111-126= H obv.; 116-121= D rev.; 127-141= E obv. ii; 131-151= C rev. iii; 158-176= I obv. and rev.; 170-175= J obv. i; 176-187= K obv. i; 179-189= L; 192-208= C rev. iv; 193-223= E rev. iii; 212-231= K obv. ii; 214-223= H rev.; 216-241= J obv. ii; 226-228= M rev. iii; 231-237= N rev. ii (i is unplaceable); 231-238= O rev.; 233-242= P obv.; 235-255= K rev. iii; 247-278= E rev. iv; 269-307= J obv. iii; 274-278= M rev. iv; 288-292= K rev. iv; 308-324= P rev.; 319-361= J rev. iv; 389-419= J rev. v; 424-459= O obv. and rev.; 491-498= R rev. i; 497-514= S obv.; 516-547= T obv. and rev.; 543-552= R rev. ii; 546-564= S rev.

TRANSLITERATION

AND

TRANSLATION

.... ki ᴋᴇ́š ....

gaba-u$_4$-da ki-nam-tar ....

unu^{ki} kur-gal šà ....

... unú-gal-an-n[a] ....

u$_4$-ri-a nam-b[a-tar-ra-a-ba]

unu^{ki} kul-aba^{ki} é-....

sag-íl-la-nun-gal-e-ne m[i]-....

ḫé-gál-a geštin-gá[l] ....

ɪᴍ-a še-gu-nu-gá[l] ....

10. unu^{ki} kul-aba^{ki}-a ....

kur-dilmun$^{[k]i}$ ....-dug$_4$

é-an-ša-[an^{ki}-na] ....-us-sa-àm

[gi$_6$]-pàr-kug .... ᴋɪ

[sig$_4$]-kul-aba^{ki} [ki]-in-dar-ra-gim ...-ag-àm

....-ɪ́ʟ bala nu-ag-e[1]

....-ɪ́ʟ nam-garàš nu-ag-e[2]

.... [n]a$_4$ urudu an-na ^{na4}lagab-za-gìn-na[3]

... [ku]r-bi-ta ur-bi[4] nu-mu-un-e$_{11}$-dè[5]

.... a nu-un-tu$_5$

20. .... mu(?)-un-dúr-ru

.... ᴜ$_4$

(Approximately three lines destroyed)

....-[d]ar

....-àm

....-gim gurun ... sig$_7$-ga-àm

^{d}inanna-ke$_4$ en-aratta^{ki}-ke$_4$

sag-men ...-ga mu-ni-in-gál

6

. . . .

The "breast of the storm," *the place where* fate . . . .

Erech, the great land, *the heart* . . . .

. . . the great shrine of Anu . . . .

[*After*] the days of *creation* [*had been*] de [*creed*],

Erech, Kullab, the house . . . .

With lifted heads, the Igigi . .

In overflow, the vine . . . . ,

In rain, the *spotted* barley . . . . ,

10. Erech, Kullab . . . . ,

The land Dilmun . . . . ,

The house of Ansh [an] . . . . ,

The holy [*gi*]*parru* . . . . ,

[The brickwork] of Kullab . . . . like a cavern,

. . . . does not *transport* . . ,

. . . . does not make . . ,

. . . . [st]one, bronze, lead, slabs *of* lapis lazuli

. . . . do not bring down *as one* from their [mount]ain,

. . . . do not bathe,

20. . . . . *dwell.*

. . . .

(Approximately three lines destroyed)

. . . .

. . . .

Like . . . . *fruit* . . . *blossoms,*

Inanna, *upon* the lord of Aratta,

Placed the . . . crown (upon his) head

30. en-kulaba-^{ki}a-gim nu-mu-na-šag$_5$

aratta^{ki} na$_4$ é-an-na mi-n [i]-...

kug-^{d}inanna-ra .... mu-un-na-dù^6

u$_4$-ba en-šà-kug-ge-pàd-da-^{d}inanna-ke$_4$

kur-z$_A$^{7}.мùš-ta šà-kug-ge-pàd-da-^{d}inanna-ke$_4$

en-me-er-kár-dumu-^{d}utu-ke$_4$

nin$_7$^{8}-a-ni^9 nin-NE-AN-...-dùg-ga

kug-^{d}inanna-ra ù-GUL mu-un-[na-gá]-gá

nin$_7$^{10}-mu-^{d}inanna unu^{ki}-š [è]^{11}

guškin ku$_5$-babbar ḫa-ma-an-galam-e

40. ^{na4}za-gìn-dur$_5$ lagab-ta ....

sù-du-ám ^{na4}za-gìn-dur$_5$ ....

unu^{ki}-ga kur-kug ....

é-an-ša-[an^{ki}-na] gub-ba-za

.... an-na ḫé-en-dù

gi$_6$-pàr-kug-g [a dúr]-gar-ra-za

šà-bi aratta^{ki} ḫa-ma-an-galam-e

mà-e šà-ba siskur .... ga-mu-...-lá

aratta [unu^{ki}-šè] gú giš ḫa-ma-[gá-gá]

nam-lú-lu$_6$^{lu}-[ar]atta^{ki}-[ke$_4$]

50. na$_4$-ḫur-sag-gá kur-[bi] ḫa-ma-ab-e$_{11}$

èš-gal ḫa-ma-dù-e u[nú]-gal ḫa-ma-gá-gá

unú-gal-unú-[dingir-re-e-ne-ke$_4$ pa]-è [ḫa]-ma-ab-ag-e

me-mu kul-aba^{ki}-[a] si ha-ma-ni-ib-sá-e

abzu kur-kug-gim ḫa-ma-ab-mú-mú

eridu^{ki} ḫur-sag-gim ḫa-ma^{12}-ab-sikil-e

èš-abzu-kug ki-in-dar-ra-gim pa-è ḫa-ma^{13}-ab-ag-e

mà-e abzu-ta zà-sal dug$_4$-ga-mu-dè

eridu^{ki}-ta me túm-a-mu-dè

nam-en-na-tán ?-bar-gim sig$_7$-ga-mu-dè

60. unu^{ki} kul-aba^{ki}-a sag-men-kug-gál-la-mu-dè^{14}

..-e-éš-gal-la-ke$_4$ gi$_6$-pàr-ra hu-mu-un^{15}-túm-mu

30. (But) did not favor him like (she favored) the lord of Kullab;

(The people of) Aratta [*brought down*] stone *for* Eanna,

Built the .... for the pure Inanna.

Once upon a time the lord chosen by Inanna in (her) holy heart,

Chosen from the land ZA.MÙŠ by Inanna in (her) holy heart,

Enmerkar, the [son] of Utu,

To his sister, the queen *of* good ....,

To the holy Inanna ma[kes] a plea:

''O my sister, Inanna, for Erech

Let them (the people of Aratta) fashion artfully gold (and) silver,

40. Let them .. pure lapis lazuli *from* the slab,

Let them .. *precious stone* (and) pure lapis lazuli;

Of Erech, the holy land ..... .

Of the house of Ansh[an] where you stand,

Let them build [its] ....;

Of the holy [*gip*]*arru* where you have established (your) [dwelling],

May (the people of) Aratta fashion artfully its interior,

I, I would *offer* prayers .... in its midst;

Let Aratta submit to Erech,

Let the people [of Ar]atta,

50. Having brought down the stones of the mountains [from their] highland,

Build for me the great chapel, set up for me the great sh[rine],

Cause to [ap]pear for me the great shrine, the shrine [of the gods],

Carry out for me my *me* [in] Kullab,

Fashion for me the Apsû like a holy highland,

Purify for me Eridu like a mountain,

Cause to appear for me the holy chapel of the Apsû like a cavern;

I, when I utter the hymns from the Apsû,

When I bring the *me* from Eridu,

When I *make blossom* the pure *ênu*-ship like a ...,

60. When I place the crown (on my) head in Erech, in Kullab,

May the .. of the great chapel *be brought* into the *giparru*,

..-e-gi$_6$-pàr-ra-ke$_4$ éš-gal-la ḫu-mu-un[16]-túm-mu

[nam]-lú-lu$_6$ u$_6$-dùg-ge[17]-eš ḫu-mu-un[18]-e

[^{d}u]tu igi- húl-la ḫé-im-ši-bar-re[19]

...-ka-zal-an-kug-ga nin-kur-ra-igi-gál

in-nin$_7$ ^{d}ama-ušumgal-an-na šim-zi-da-ni

^{d}inanna-nin-kur-kur-ra-ke$_4$

en-me-er-kár-dumu-^{d}utu-ra gù mu-na-dé-e

en-me-er-kár gá-nu na ga-e-ri na-ri-mu ḫé-e-díb

70.   inim ga-ra-ab-dug$_4$ [gizz]al ḫé-ši-ag

kin-gi$_4$-a-inim-zu zag-še ...-ta [ù-b]a-[e-r]e-pàd

inim-gal-^{d}inanna-gal[20]-zu-inim-ma-ke$_4$ me-a ḫu-mu-na-ab-tùm(?)

ḫur-sag-?-šè ḫé[21]-bí-e$_{11}$-dè

ḫur-sag-?-ta[22] ḫé[23]-im-ma-da-ra-e$_{11}$-dè

dar-?-ki[24]-e-kur-an-ša-an^{ki}-a-šè

nar[25]-tur[26]-gim ka šu ḫu-mu-na-ab-gál[27]

ḫur-sag-gal-gal-ní-ba-[lu]-a

saḫar-ra ḫu-mu[28]-na-da-[ni]gin-e

aratta^{ki} unu^{ki}-šè gu giš ma-gá-gá

80.   nam-lú-lu$_6$-aratta^{ki}-ke$_4$

na$_4$-ḫur-sag-gá kur-bi um-ta-ab-e$_{11}$

éš-gal ḫa-ra-dù-e unú-gal ḫa-ra-gá-gá

unú-gal-unu-dingir-re-e-ne-ke$_4$ pa-è ḫa-ra-ab-ag-e

me-zu kul-aba^{ki}-a si ḫa-ra-ni-íb[29]-sá-e

abzu kur-kug-gim ḫa-ra-ab-mú-mú

eridu^{ki} ḫur-sag-gim ḫa-ra-ab-sikil-e

éš-abzu-kug ki-dar-ra-gim pa-è ḫa-ra-ab-ag-e

za-e abzu-ta zà-sal-dug$_4$-ga-zu-dè

eridu^{ki}-ta me-túm-a-[zu-dè]

90.   nam-en-tán-na ?-bar-[gim sig$_7$-ga]-zu-dè

unu^{ki}-kul-aba^{ki}-a [sag-men-kug-gál-la]-zu-dè

[?-e][30]-éš-gal-la-ke$_4$ [gi$_6$-pàr-ra] ḫu-mu-un-túm-mu

[?-e-gi$_6$-pàr-ra-ke$_4$ é]š-gal-la ḫu-mu-un-túm-mu

May the .. of the *giparru be brought* into the great chapel,

May the [pe]ople admire approvingly,

May [U]tu look on with joyful eye."

She who is ... the delight of holy Anu, the queen who eyes the highland,

The *mistress* whose kohl is Amaushumgalanna,

Inanna, the queen of all the lands,

Says to Enmerkar, the son of Utu:

"Come, Enmerkar, instruction I would offer you, take my instruction,

70. A word I would speak to you, give ear to it!

Choose a word-wise herald from ...,

Let the great words of the word-wise Inanna be *brought* to him in ..,

Let him ascend the .. mountains,

Let him descend the .. mountains,

Before the .. of Anshan,

Let him prostrate himself like a young singer,

Awed by the dread of the great mountains,

Let him wander about in the dust —

Aratta will submit to Erech;

80. The people of Aratta,

Having brought down the stones of the mountains from their land,

Will build for you the great chapel, set up for you the great shrine,

Cause to appear for you the great shrine, the shrine of the gods,

Carry out for you your *me* in Kullab,

Fashion for you the Apsû like a holy highland,

Purify for you Eridu like a mountain,

Cause to appear for you the holy chapel of the Apsû like a cavern;

You, when you utter the hymns from the Apsû,

[When you] bring the *me* from Eridu,

90. When you *make blossom* the pure *ènu*-ship [like] a ...,

When you [place the crown (on your) head] in Erech, in Kullab,

The .. of the great chapel will *be brought* [into the *giparru*],

[The .. of the *giparru*] will *be brought* into the great [ch]apel.

[nam-lú-lu₆] u₆-dùg-ge-eš ḫé-mu-e-e

[ᵈuti i]gi-ḫúl-la ḫé-mu-e-ši-bar-bar-re

[nam]-lú-lu₆-ar [attaᵏⁱ-]ke₄

...-ɴᴇ u₄-šú-uš-ta ....-eš

..-ɴᴇ u₄-te-en-e ....

ki-ᵈdumu-zi-da ganam máš .... ù(?)-a(?)

100. a-kalag-ga a-šà-ᵈdumu-zi-da-ka

udu-kur-ra-gim dùg ḫa-ra-ni-ib-gar

gaba-kug-é-a u₄-gim-è-ni

?-ág-gá níg-mùš-bi ḫé-me-en

.... en-me-er-kár-dumu-ᵈutu zà-sal

en-e inim-[kug-ᵈinann]a-ka-šè sag-kéš ba-ši-in-ag

kin-gi₄-a-inim-zu zag-še ...[-ta] ba-ra-an-pàd[31]

inim-gal-ᵈinanna-gal-zu-inim-ma-ke₄ me-a[32] mu[33]-na-ab-tùm(?)

ḫur-sag-?-ka ḫé-bí-in-e₁₁-dè-en

ḫur-sag-?-ta ḫé-im-ma-da-ra-an-e₁₁-dè-en

110. dar-?-ki-e-[kur-an]-ša₄-anᵏⁱ-a-šè

nar-tur[34]-gim ka šu ḫu-mu-na-ab-gál

ḫur-sag-gal-gal-ní-ba-lu-a

saḫar-ra ḫu-mu-na-da-nigin-e[35]

kin-gi₄-a en-arattaᵏⁱ-ra[36] ù-na[37]-dug₄ ù-na[38]-dè-daḫ[39]

uru-bi[40] ᴋᴀs-sag-ᵐᵘˢᵉⁿgim[41] giš-bi-ta na-an-na-ra-ab-dal-en[42]

mušen-gim gùd-ús-sa-bi-a nam-bí-ib-dal-le(?)-en[43]

ki-lam-gál-la-gim na-an-si-ig-en[44]

uru-gul-gul-lu[45]-gim saḫar nam-bí-ib-ḫa-za-en[46]

arattaᵏⁱ á-dam ᵈen-ki-ke₄ nam-ba-an-tar

120. ki-bí-in-gul-la-gim ki(?) nam-ga-bí-ib-gul-e[47]

egir-bi ᵈinanna ba-ši-in-zi

ᴋᴀ i[m-mi-in-ra-e₁₁ im]-mi-in-gi₄[48]

saḫar b[í-in-su-a-gim sa]ḫar nam-ga-bí-ib-su-su

guškin ù-tu-da-ba-.... a-ba-ni-in-ag

kug-me-a s[aḫar-ba] zag ù-ba-ni-in-uš

[The people] will admire approvingly,

[Utu] will look on with joyful eye;

The people of Aratta,

.... daily ....,

.... evening ....,

In the place of Dumuzi, ewes, kid ....,

100. *The mighty seed, the seed (implanted) in the womb by Dumuzi,*

Will bend the knee before you like highland sheep;

O holy '*breast*' of the house, whose coming out is like the sun,

You are the .. of the ..-

O .... Enmerkar, son of Utu, praise!''

The lord gave heed to the word of the [holy Inan]na,

Chose a word-wise herald [from] ...,

Brought to him the great words of the word-wise Inanna in ..:

''Ascend the ..-mountains,

Descend the ..-mountains,

110. Before the .. of Anshan,

Prostrate yourself like a young singer,

Awed by the dread of the great mountains,

Wander about in the dust —

O herald, speak unto the lord of Aratta (and) say unto him:

'I will make (the people of) that city flee like the ..-bird from its tree,

I will make them flee like a bird into its neighboring nest,

I will make it (Aratta) *desolate* like a place of ...,

I will make it *hold* dust like an utterly destroyed city,

Aratta, that habitation (which) Enki has cursed —

120. I will surely destroy *the place*, like *a place* which has been destroyed,

Inanna *has risen (up in arms) behind it,*

[*Has brought down*] *the word, has turned it back,*

Like the *heaped up* dust, I will surely *heap* dust upon it;

Having *made* ... gold in its *ore*,

Pressed ..-silver [in its] dust,

kug-sag-PA-TÚG ù-mu-un-dím-dím

anšu-kur-[kur]-ra-ke₄ bara um-mi-in-lá-lá

é-a⁴⁹-hun-àm-ᵈen-líl-bàn-da-ki-en-gi-ra-ke₄

en-ᵈnu-dím-mud⁵⁰-šà-kug-ge-pàd-da

130. kur-me-sikil-la-ke₄⁵¹ ha-ma-dù-e

ᵍⁱˢtaškarin-gim hi-li ha-ma-ab-ag-e

ᵈutu-gán-nun⁵²-ta-è-a-gim si múš ha-ma-ab-dar-dar

zag-du₈-zag-du₈-bi šeš ha-ma-mul-e

gán-nun-gán-nun-ba sìr-kug nam-šub tuku-a-ba⁵³

nam-šub-ᵈnu-dím-mud-da-ke₄⁵⁴ e-ne-ra dug₄-mu-na-ab

u₄-ba muš nu-gál-àm⁵⁵ gír nu-gál-àm⁵⁶

ka nu-gál-àm ur-mah nu-gál-àm⁵⁷

ur-zír ur-bar-ra nu-gál-àm⁵⁸

ní-te-gá su-zi-zi-i nu-gál-àm⁵⁹

140. lú-lu₆ gaba-šu-gar nu-tuku⁶⁰

u₄-ba kur-šubur [ki-ha]-ma-zíᵏⁱ⁶¹

eme-ha-mun ki-en-gi kur-gal-me-nam-nun-na-ka

ki-uri kur-me-te-gál-la

kur-mar-tu ú-sal-la-ná-a

an-ki-nigín-na uku-sag-sì-ga

ᵈen-líl-ra eme-aš-àm hé-en-na-da-[si-il]

u₄-ba a-da-en a-da-nun a-da-luga[l]

ᵈen-ki a-da-en a-da-nun a-da-lug[al]

a-da-en- NE a-da-nun-NE a-da-lu[gal-NE]

150. .... hé-gál-la-dug₄-ga ....

....

....

....

.... [unu]ᵏⁱ-ga ...

....-en-na mi-ni-in-...

..-nam-lú-lu₆ ....

mìn-kam-ma-šè en-e kin-gi₄-a-kur-šè-du-úr

Fashioned silver ...,

Fastened the *crates* on the mountain-asses —

The ... house of Sumer's junior Enlil,

Chosen by the lord Nudimmud in (his) holy heart,

130. Let (the people of) the highland of pure *me* build for me,

Make it *flower* for me like the *boxwood*-tree,

Light it up for me like Utu coming out of the *ganunnu*,

Adorn for me its thresholds';

Of its *ganunnu's*, its holy song (*and*) spell,

The spell of Nudimmud pronounce unto him:

'Once upon a time there was no snake, there was no scorpion,

There was no *hyena*, there was no lion,

There was no *wild dog*, no wolf,

There was no fear, no terror,

140. Man had no rival.

Once upon a time the lands Shubur (and) [Ha]mazi,

Many-tongued Sumer, the great land of the decrees of princeship,

Uri, the land having (all) that is *appropriate*,

The land Martu, resting in security,

The whole universe, the people *in unison*,

To Enlil in one tongue [*gave praise*].

In those days, the father the lord, the father the prince, the father the king,

Enki, the father the lord, the father the prince, the father the king,

The father the .. lord, the father the .. prince, the father the .. king,

150. .... abundance ....,

.....

.....

.... in [Erech] ....

.....

.. man .....' "

A second time the lord, to the herald journeying to the highland,

aratta^ki-aš inim mu-na-ab-daḫ-e

kin-gi₄-a gi₆-ù-na-ka ɪᴍ-diš-gim šèg-gá

160. an-ne-ɢÁɴ-ka ɪᴍ-ɢᴀʙᴀ-gim zi-ga

kin-gi₄-a inim-lugal-la-na-ke₄ sag-kéš ba-ši-in-ag⁶²

gi₆-ù-na-ka mul-àm im-du

an-ne-ɢÁɴ-ka ^dutu-an-na-ta mu-un-dè⁶³-du

inim-gal-^dinanna-gi-su₁₁-lum-ma-na⁶⁴ me-a mu-na-ab-tùm

ḫur-sag-?-šè bi-in-e₁₁-dè

ḫur-sag-?-ta im-ma-da-ra-ab-e₁₁-dè

dar-?-ki-e-kur-an-ša₄-an^ki-a-šè

nar-tur-[gi]m ka šu mu-na-ab-gál

ḫur-sag-gal-gal-ní-ba-lu-a

170. saḫar-ra mu-na-da-nigin⁶⁵

ḫur-sag-ìa ḫur-sag-àš ḫur-sag-imin im-me-re-bal-bal

[igi mu-un-í]l aratta^ki-aš ba-te

[kisal-aratt]a^ki-ka gír-ḫúl-la mi-ni⁶⁶-gub

nam-nir-gál-lugal-a-na mu-un-zu

búr-ra-bi inim-šà-ga-na bí⁶⁷-ib-be

kin-gi₄-a en-aratta^ki-ra⁶⁸ mu-na-ab-bal-e

a-a-[z]u lugal-mu mu-e-ši-in-gi₄-in⁶⁹-nam

[en-unu^ki]-ga en-kul-aba^ki-a-ke₄ mu-e-ši-in-gi₄-nam

lugal-za dug₄-ga-ni nam-mu daḫ-a-ni nam-mu

180. lugal-mu a-na bí-in-dug₄ a-n[a bi-in-daḫ]-àm⁷⁰

lugal-mu ù-tu-da-ni-ta men-na-du-ma

en-unu^ki-ga muš⁷¹-sag-kal-ki-en-gi-ra kur-šè-gim⁷²-dug₄-dug₄

šenbar kur-bàd-da á-nun-gál

tùr-za⁷³-maš-ᴇʟᴛᴇɢ-kug-ga dubbin ....-e

áb-zi-da⁷⁴-kur-šà-ga-tu-da

en-me-er-kár-dumu-^dutu-ke₄ mu-e-ši-in-gi₄-nam⁷⁵

lugal-mu na-ab-b[e]-a

uru-ni ᴋᴀs-sag-^mušengim giš-bi-ta [n]a-ra-a[b-dal-en]

mušen-gim gud-us-sa-bi-a na-an-bi-i[b-d]al-[le(?)]-en

To Aratta, says:

"O herald, during the night .. like a .. ,

160. During the day, rise up like ..."

The herald gave heed to the word of his king.

During the night he journeyed by the stars,

During the day he journeyed with Utu of heaven,

The great words of Inanna .... *were brought* unto him in .. ,

He ascends the ..-mountains,

He descends the ..-mountains,

Before the .. of Anshan,

He prostrated himself like a young singer,

Awed by the dread of the great mountains,

170. He wandered about in the dust;

Five mountains, six mountains, seven mountains he crossed,

[Lif]ted (his) [eyes], approached Aratta,

In the [court-yard of Arat]ta he set a joyous foot,

Made known the exaltedness of his king,

Spoke reverently the word of his heart.

The herald says to the lord of Aratta:

"Your father, my king, has sent me to you,

[The lord] of [Erech], the lord of Kullab, has sent me to you."

"Your king, *what* has he spoken, *what* has he said?"

180. "My king, this is what he has spoken, this is what he has said —

My king fit for the crown from his (very) birth,

The lord of Erech, the leading serpent of Sumer, who ... like a .. ,

The ram full of princely might *in the walled highland,*

The *shepherd* who .... ,

Born of the faithful cow in the heart of the highland —

Enmerkar, the son of Utu, has sent me to you,

My king, this is what he says:

'I will make (the people of) his city flee like the ..-bird from its tree,

I will make them flee like a bird into its neighboring nest,

190. ki-lam-gál-la-gim na-an-si-ge-en

uru-gul-gul-lu-dè(!) na-an-bí-[ib-ḫa-za]-en

aratta^{ki} á-dam-^{d}en-ki-ke$_4$ nam-ba(?)-an(?)-tar

ki-bí-in-gul-la-gim ki(?) nam-ga-bí-ib-gul-en

egir-bi ^{d}inanna ba-ši-in-zi

ᴋᴀ im-mi-in[76]-ra-e$_{11}$ im-mi-in-gi$_4$

saḫar bí-in-su-a-gim saḫar na-an-ga-bí-ib-su-su-un

guškin ù-tu-da-ba .... a-ba-ni-in-ag

kug-me-a saḫar-ba zag ù-ba-ni-in-uš

kug-sag-ᴘᴀ-ᴛúɢ[77] ù-mu-un-dím-dím

200. anšu-kur-kur-ra-ke$_4$ bara[78] um-mi-in-lá-lá

é-a[79]-hun-àm-^{d}en-líl-bàn-da-ki-en-gi-ra-ke$_4$

en-^{d}nu-dím-mud-e šà-kug-ge-pàd-da[80]

kur-me-sikil-la-ke$_4$[81] ḫa-ma-dù-e

^{giš}taškarin-gim ḫi-li ḫa-ma-ab-ag[82]

^{d}utu-gán-nun-ta-è-a-gim si múš ḫa-ma-ab-dar-dar[83]

[zag-d]u$_8$-zag-du$_8$-bi[84] šᴇš ḫa-ma-mul-e

[gán-nun-gán-n]un-ba sìr-kug nam-šub tuku-a-ba[85]

[nam-šub-^{d}nu]-dím-mud-[da-kam e-ne]-ra dug$_4$-[mu-na-ab]

a-na-ma-ab[86]-be-en-na-bi [ù-mu-e-dug$_4$]

210. a-ru-a su$_6$-^{na_4}za-gìn-[sù(?)-da-ar]

áb-kal-la[87]-ga-ni kur-me-sikil-la ᴋᴀ-[kéš-da-ar]

saḫar-aratta^{ki}-ka[88] a-è-[a-ar]

amaš-áb-zi-da-ka ga-kú-[a-ar]

kul-aba^{ki}[89] kur-me-gal[90]-gal-la-ka nam-en-na-du-ma

en-me-er-kár-dumu-^{d}utu-ra[91]

inim-bi èš-é-an-na-ka inim-dùg[92] ga[93]-na-ab-dug$_4$

gi$_6$-pàr-^{giš}teḫi-gibil-gim gurun[94]-íl-la-na

lugal-mu en-kul-aba^{ki}-ra šu-a[95] ga-mu-na-ab-gi$_4$

ḫur-gim ḫu-mu-na-ab-be-a-ka

220. kin-gi$_4$-a lugal-zu en-kul-aba^{ki}-a[96]-ra ù-na-dug$_4$ ù-na-dè-taḫ

mà-e-me-en en-šu-sikil-la-du-ma[97]

190. I will make it *desolate* like a place of . . . ,

I will make it *hold* dust like an utterly destroyed city,

Aratta, that habitation (which) Enki has cursed —

I will surely destroy *the place* like *a place* which has been destroyed,

Inanna *has risen (up in arms) behind it*,

Has brought down the word, has turned it back,

Like the *heaped up* dust, I will surely *heap* dust upon it;

Having *made* . . . gold in its *ore*,

Pressed . .-silver in its dust,

Fashioned silver . . . ,

200. Fastened the *crates* on the mountain-asses —

The . . . house of Sumer's junior Enlil,

Chosen by the lord Nudimmud in (his) holy heart,

Let (the people of) the highland of pure *me* build for me,

Make it *flower* for me like the *boxwood*-tree

Light it up for me like Utu coming out of the *ganunnu*,

Adorn for me its thresholds';

Of its *ganunnu*'s, its holy song (*and*) spell,

[The spell of Nu]dimmud pron[ounce unto him];

[Command] what I shall say concerning this matter,

210. (And) to the dedicated one who *wears a long* beard of lapis lazuli,

[To him] whose mighty cow . . s the land of pure *me*

[To him] whose seed came forth in the dust of Aratta,

[To him] who was fed milk in the fold of the faithful cow,

[To him who was fit] for lordship *over* Kullab, the land of all the great *me*

To Enmerkar, the son of Utu,

[I will speak] that word as a good word in the temple of Eanna;

In the *giparru* which bears [fruit] like a fresh . .-plant,

I will deliver it to my king, the lord of Kullab."

After he had thus spoken to him,

220. "O herald, speak unto your king, the lord of Kullab, and say unto him:

'Me, the lord fit for the pure hand,

giš-lugal[98]-an-na nin-an-ki-a[99]-ke$_4$

in-nin$_7$-me-šár-ra kug-^{d}inanna-ke$_4$

aratta^{ki}-kur-me-sikil-la-šè ḫu-mu-un-túm-en

kur-ra ^{giš}ig-gal-gim igi-ba bí-in-tab-en

aratta^{ki} unu^{ki}-šè gú a-gim i-gá-gá

aratta^{ki} unu^{ki}-šè gú-gá-gá nu-gál e-ne-ra dug$_4$-mu-na-ab

ḫur-gim ḫu-mu-na-ab-be-a-ka

kin-gi$_4$-a en-aratta^{ki}-ra mu-na-ni-ib-gi$_4$-gi$_4$[100]

230. nin-gal-an-na[101] me-ḫuš-a-u$_5$-a

ḫur-sag-kur-ZA.[102]MÙŠ-ka dúr-gar-ra

bara-kur-ZA.[103]MÙŠ-ka še-ir-ka-an-dug$_4$-ga

en-lugal-mu šubur-a-ni-im

^{d}nin-é-an-na-ka[104] mu-un-di-ni-ib-tu-re-eš[105]

en-aratta^{ki} gú ki-šè[106] ba-ni-in-gál[107]

sig$_4$-kul-aba^{ki}-a[108]-ka ḫur-gim ḫu-mu-na-ab-bé-en[109]

u$_4$-bi-a[110] en-e šà mu-un-sìg zi mu-un-ir-ir

gaba-ri nu-mu[111]-da-gál gaba-ri i-kin-kin

gìr-ní-te-a[112]-na-ka igi-lib[113]-ba bí-in-gaba-ru gaba-ri ì[114]-pàd-dè

240. gaba-ri in-pàd[115] inim im-ta-an-è[116]

kin-gi$_4$-a inim-ma gaba-ri-bi

gud-gim gù-nun mu-un-di-ni-ib-be[117]

[kin-gi$_4$-a lugal]-zu-en-kul-aba^{ki}-a[118]-ra [ù]-na-dug$_4$ ù-na-dè-daḫ

.... an-da-mú-a

..-bi .... -ra-àm PA-bi[119] giš-búr-àm[120]

.... [d]$_{IM-MI}$^{mušen} ḫu-rí-in-na[121]

la ... ^{d}inanna DÙG KA gil-ba[122]

?-úr-ḫu-rí-in-na^{mušen}-bi[123] ù-mun-kúr-ra[124] kur-MÙŠ-e$_{11}$[125]

aratta^{ki}-a ír ....[126]

250. a-bal-bal-àm zíd-dub-dub-ba-àm[127]

kur-ra zur-zur-a-ra-zu-a[128] ka-šu-gál-la-àm

lú-ía nu-me-a lú-u nu-me-a

unu^{ki}-zi-ga ḫur-sag-?-šè sag a-gim ì-gá-gá

She who is the royal .. of heaven, the queen of heaven and earth,

The *mistress* of all the *me*, the holy Inanna;

Has brought me to Aratta, the land of pure *me*,

Has made me close "the face of the highland" like a large door;

How then shall Aratta submit to Erech!

Aratta will not submit to Erech' — say unto him.''

After he had thus spoken to him,

The herald answers the lord of Aratta:

230. ''The great queen of heaven, who rides the fearful *me*,

Who dwells in the mountains of the highland ZA.MÙŠ

Who *adorns* the daises of the highland ZA.MÙŠ —

Because the lord, my king, who is her *servant*,

Made her the 'Queen of Eanna.'

'The lord of Aratta *will* submit' —

Thus said to him in the brickwork of Kullab.''

Then was the lord depressed, deeply pained,

He had no answer, he kept seeking an answer,

At his own feet he *cast* a troubled eye, he finds an answer.

240. He found an answer, he uttered the word,

At the herald, the answer to the word,

Like an ox he roared:

''[O herald], speak unto your [king], the lord of Kullab, and say unto him:

'.... *growing towards heaven*

Its (*root*) is a ...., its *crown* is a *giš burru*

.... the Zu-bird, the Ḥurin-bird,

.... Inanna ....,

... its Ḥurin-bird which *brings down the blood of the enemy* ....

In Aratta, *tears* ....,

250. Water is poured, flour is sprinkled,

In the highland there are sacrifices, prayers, and prostrations;

How, then, without five men, without ten men,

Does the rebellious Erech *plot* against the .. mountain!'

lugal-zu ^{giš}tukul-? sag ḫa-ba-an-sì

mà-e a-da-man-na sag g[a-b]a-an-sì

a-da-man nu-um-zu ur [nu-um]-kú

gud-dè gud-da-gál-bi [nu-um-z]u

[a-da-ma]n um-zu ur um-[kú]

[gud-d]è gud-da-gál-bi um-z[u]

260.   . . . a-da-man mi-ni-in-KÍD-KÍD-an[129]

. . . níg lú nu-sì-ge[130]

. .-NE in-ga-mu-ni-in-KÍD-KÍD-an

. .-ma-šè kin-gi$_4$-a inim mu-ra-bé-en[131]

. . dé-a ša-ra-ab-galam-e[132]-en du[133]-a ḫé-mu-e-ši-díb[134]

é-an-na UG šu ba-ná-a

šà-bi-ta gud$_4$[135]-gù-nun-di-dam

gi$_6$-pàr ^{giš}teḫi-gibil-gim gurun-íl-la-na

lugal-zu en-kul-aba^{ki}-a[136]-ra šu-a gi$_4$-mu-na-ab[137]

ḫur-sag ur-KA-galam-si-ga-àm

270. ^{d}usán-na é-bi-šè du-gim[138]

igi-bi-ta BAD-lá-lá-e[139]-gim

^{d}nanna si-BÀD-na maḫ-a-gim

sag-ki-bi me-lám-gál-la-gim

giš-gim kur-kur-ra gil-ba-bi

sag-MÙŠ-aratta^{ki}-ke$_4$[140]

^{d}lama-šag$_5$-ga kur-me-sikil-la-šè[141]

u$_4$-da aratta^{ki} aga-kug-an-na[142]-gim si mu-na-an-sá[143]

mà-e u$_4$-ba nam-maḫ-mu ga-an-zu[144]

še bara-ga nam-mu-un-si-si-ig-ge mar-e nam-me[145]-e

280.   še-bi kur-kur-ra nam-íl-e[146]

erín-na mu[147]-un-TAR nam-mu-un-gá-gá

še sa-al-kad$_5$-e ù-mu-ni-in-si-si

anšu-bara-lá-e um-mi-in-lá

anšu-bal-e[148] da-bi-a a-ba-an-sì

tukum-bi kisal-aratta^{ki}-ka gur$_7$-šè mu[149]-dub-ba

Your king has resorted to .. weapons,

I will resort to the contest —

Who 'knows' not the contest, has not devoured,

The ox 'knows' not the ox at its side,

Who 'knows' the contest

The ox 'knows' the ox at its side —

260. *... I shall ..* the contest,

... which none can equal,

... I shall indeed *..*,

... O herald, I say a word to you,

... I speak artfully to you, hold it before you in *..*,

In Eanna where the lion lies on its paws,

From whose midst the ox roars,

In his *giparru* which bears fruit like a new ..-plant,

Deliver it to your king, the lord of Kullab.

'The mountain, *the warrior who attacks with artful word,*

270. Who like Dusk coming home,

Like (Dusk) from whose face *blood drips,*

Like Nanna high in the *upper sky,*

Like (Nanna) whose forehead is *ray-filled,*

Like a tree it stands athwart the lands —

When the ... of Aratta,

(For) the kindly *lamassu*, unto the highland of the pure *me,*

Directs Aratta *for him* like heaven's holy crown,

Then would I make known my pre-eminence,

I will pour the grain into the *crates, I ....*,

280. *I* will carry that grain *into* the lands,

I will set up *....*,

If, having poured grain into the sacks,

Loaded them on the *crate*-carrying donkeys,

Placed them on the sides of the *transporting* donkeys;

He will have heaped it up in the courtyard of Aratta *for* the storehouse —

NI-ge[150] ÀM-dub-bi gur$_7$-a ḫi-li-bi

kur-kur-re [151] NE-gar-ra-bi á-dam me-te-bi[152]

bàd-imin-e še-ir-ka-an-dug$_4$-ga

nin-ur-sag mé-a-du-ma

290. ^{d}inanna-ur-sag mé-saḫar-ra[153]-ka sag-ešemen[154] di-dam

NI-ge-en-aratta^{ki} ur-du$_{14}$-mú[155] šu-ta um[156]-ta-ri

mà-e u$_4$-ba ša-ba[157]-na-gam-e-dè-en

e-ne nam-maḫ-a-ni ši-im-ma-an-zu-zu-un

uru-gim nam-tur-mà[158] gú ši-im-ma-gá-gá-an e-ne-ra dug$_4$-mu-na-ab

ḫur-gim ḫu-mu-na-ab-be-[a-ka][159]

kin-gi$_4$-a-en-aratta^{ki}-ke$_4$

ka-zal-gim inim ka-na ba-an-sì

SUN-gim ḫaš-a-na mu-un-gur

nim-saḫar-ra-gim tir u$_4$-zal-le-na mu-un-túm

300. sig$_4$-kul-aba^{ki}-ka gìr-ḫúl-la mu-ni-in-gub

kisal-maḫ-e kisal-gú-en-na-ka kin-gi$_4$-a i-íb[160]-búr

lugal-a-ni-ir en-kul-aba^{ki}-[ra][161]

ka-zal-gim šu mu-na-an-gi$_4$

gud-gim inim mu-na-an-sì

gud-ri-ri[162]-gim geštug mu-na-an-[sì]

lugal-e zag-zi-da-ni-dè im-mi-in-t[uš]

zag-gùb-bu-ni im-ma-ni-in-gi$_4$

NI-ge-en-aratta^{ki} ?-sì-ma im-ma-zu im-me

u$_4$ im-zal ^{d}utu im-ta-è-a-ra

310. ^{d}utu kalam-ma-ka sag nu-un-íl

lugal(!)-e ^{íd}idiglat ^{íd}buranun-bi-d[a] im-ma-da-an-tab

^{íd}buranun-na ^{íd}idiglat-da im-ma-da-an-tab

bur-gal-gal an-ne ba-su$_8$-su$_8$-ug

bur-tur-tur sila$_4$-ú-šim-díb-gim zag-bi-a im-ma-an-uš

bur-i-gi$_8$[163]-an-na da-bi-a ba-su$_8$-ug

lugal-e eš-da-guškin-ga-ke$_4$

Then, since (she who is) the *abundance of wealth*, the flourishing of the

storehouse,

The beacon of all the lands, the *vital need* of the people,

Who adorns the seven walls,

The queen, the heroine fit for battle,

290. Inanna, the heroine, who *dances for joy in the dust of battle*,

Has *taken* from (*my*) hand the *wealth* of Aratta, like a quarrelsome enemy,

I will bow down to him;

He will make known to me his pre-eminence,

Like the city I will submit in my *smallness*,' say unto him.''

[After] he had thus spoken to him,

The herald of the lord of Aratta,

Delightedly put the word in his mouth,

Like a wild cow he turned upon his thigh,

Like the dust-fly he *brought* the . . . ,

300. In the brickwork of Erech he set a joyous foot,

At the lofty courtyard, in the courtyard of the assembly hall explained it,

Unto his king, the lord of Kullab,

Delightedly delivered *it*.

Like an ox he gave him the word,

Like an . . ox [*he gave*] ear to him.

The king seated him at his right side,

His left side *he turned*,

The *wealth* of Aratta, the . . . , *he made known, he recited.*

Day broke; unto the risen Utu,

310. *Unto* Utu of the land he lifted not (his) head,

The king *joined* the Tigris with the Euphrates,

He *joined* the Euphrates with the Tigris.

Large jars he made stand heavenward,

Small jars, like lambs *holding* plants and herbs, he leaned against them,

Lead . .-jars he stationed at their side;

The king, *at* the . . of gold,

en-me-er-kár-dumu-^{d}utu-ke$_4$ dùg mu-un-bad-bad-du

u$_4$-bi-a dub-i-gi$_8$ ^{164} im-me-a gi-KAK-ukkin-na

alan-guškin-ga u$_4$-dùg-ga-tu-da

320. AN-^{d}nidaba-sig$_7$-ga ?-sikil-tu-da

^{d}nidaba nin-geštug-dagal-la-ke$_4$

é-geštug-^{d}nidaba-kug-ga-ni ig ba-na-an-kíd

é-gal-an-na-ka ^{165} tu-ra-ni geštug mu-un-gá-gá

en-e gán-nun-maḫ-a-ni ig ba-an-kíd

li ^{166}-id-ga-maḫ-a-ni ki b[a-an]-uš

lugal-e še-ta še-libir-ra-ni ba-ra-an-[è]

bulùg ki-šár-ra-a ba-ni-in-..

?-bi ^{ú}kankal-ḫu-rí-in . . . .

sa-al-kad$_5$-e igi im-mi-in-tur-tur

330. še gur$_7$ KA i-ni-in-si KA bur^{mušen}-e ^{167} bí ^{168}-in-daḫ

anšu-bara ^{169}-lá-e um-mi-in-lá

anšu-bal-e ^{170} da-bi-a ba-an-sì

lugal en-geštug-dagal-la-ke$_4$

en-unu^{ki}-ga en-kul-aba^{ki}-ke$_4$

ḫar-ra-an ^{171}-aratta^{ki}-ke$_4$ ^{172} si bi-in-sá

nam-lú-lu$_6$ ^{173} kiši$_6$-ki-in-dar-ra-gim ^{174}

aratta^{ki}-aš ní-ba mu-un-su$_8$-be-eš

en-e kin-gi$_4$-a kur-se-du-úr

aratta^{ki}-aš inim mu-na-ab-daḫ-e

340. kin-gi$_4$-a en-aratta^{ki}-ra ù-na ^{175}-dug$_4$ ù-na-dè-daḫ

gidru-mà úr-bi me-nam-nun-na-ka

gidru-bi kul-aba^{ki}-a ^{176} an-dùl-eš ì-ag ^{177}

gidru-mul-mul-la-bi éš-é-an-na-ke$_4$ ^{178}

kug-^{d}inanna-ke$_4$ ní im-ši-ib-te-en-te

gidru um-ta-an-kíd ^{179} ḫu-mu-un ^{180}-gál

$^{na}_4$gug giš-aš $^{na}_4$za-gìn giš-aš-gim šu-ni-a ḫu-mu-un ^{181}-gál

en-aratta^{ki}-ke$_4$ igi ^{182}-mu-šè ḫu-mu-un-túm ^{183} e-ne-ra dug$_4$-mu-na-ab

ḫur-gim ḫu-mu-na-ab-bé-a-ka

Enmerkar, the son of Utu, *hurries about.*

Then-- the tablet of . . . ., the reed nail *of the assembly,*

The gold statue fashioned on a favorable day,

320. The *goddess* Nidaba, *the well-formed,* fashioned *of* pure . . ,

The goddess Nidaba, the lady of great wisdom —

He opened the door of his holy wisdom-house of Nidaba;

Upon entering Anu's palace, he gives ear.

The lord (then) opened the door of his lofty *ganunnu,*

He stepped up to his lofty *silo,*

The king brought out his old grain from the grain,

. . d *groats throughout,*

. . d, *its* . . , the . .-plant *of* the Ḫurin-bird,

Eyed closely the sacks,

330. Poured into them the grain *for* the storehouse, *added* . . . . .

Having loaded them on the *crate*-carrying donkeys,

Having placed them on the sides of the *transporting* donkeys,

The king, the lord of great wisdom,

The lord of Erech, the lord of Kullab,

Directed them on the road to Aratta;

The people, like ants in their holes,

Proceeded to Aratta *in fear.*

The lord, to the herald journeying to the highland,

To Aratta, says:

340. "O herald, speak unto the lord of Aratta and say unto him:

'My scepter, the *base* of which is the *me* of princeship,

That scepter has been a protecting-shade over Kullab,

That all-bright scepter, in the shrine Eanna,

Of the holy Inanna, *has banished all fear.*

Having . . d the scepter, let him place,

Carnelian (like) *one tree,* lapis lazuli like *one tree,* let him place in his hand,

Let the lord of Aratta bring before me,' say unto him.''

After he had thus spoken to him,

kin-gi$_4$-a aratta^{ki}-aš du-ni

350. saḫar-kaskal-la gìr-ni mu-un-si

na$_4$-tur-tur-ḫur-sag-gá-ke$_4$ [184] suḫ-suḫ mu-un-da-ab-za

ušumgal-edin-na-ba-kin-gá-gim gaba-ri nu-mu-ni-in-tuku

kin-gi$_4$-a aratta^{ki}-aš um-ma-te-a-ra

nam-lú-lu$_6$ [185]-aratta^{ki}-ke$_4$

anšu-bara-lá-e u$_5$-di-dè im-ma-súg-súg-ge-eš

kin-gi$_4$-a kisal-aratta^{ki}-ka [186]

še gur$_7$ KA bí-in-si KA bur$_5$^{mušen}-e [187] bí-in-daḫ

seg$_7$-a-an-na u$_4$-gál-la-gim

aratta^{ki} ḫé-gál-la [188] ì-dù [189]

360. AN-TUš-bé-a ba-da-ab-gi$_4$-a-gi [m]

aratta^{ki} šà-gar-ra-ni àm-lá-[lá]

nam-lú-lu$_6$-aratta^{ki}-[ke$_4$]

bulùg-a-si-ga-na a-šà mu-ni-...

egir-ba rá-gaba šà ....

... ki-a-KÍD-ba ....

....

.... NI ....

... aratta^{ki} giš ....

aratta^{ki}-aš KA mu-un-..

370. ḪUR-da aratta^{ki}-a šu-ta ....

en-unu^{ki}-ga-ra šu-ni i-im-....

me-en-dè sù-ga lul-la-b [i-šè]

en-kul-aba^{ki}-a-ra ^{na_4}gug l[ul-la-me-a] ga-mu-na-dúr-ru-dè-en-dè-e [n]

ab-ba-ab-ba-inim-zu-ne

šu ur-a bí-ib-RI-... zag-é-gar$_8$-e bí-ib-...

en-ra é-sikil-bi ḫu-mu-un-gá-gá

.... DU-DU šà-é-....

[búr-ra-bi inim-šà-ga]-na bí-[ib-bé]

[a-a-zu lugal-mu] mu-e-ši-i[n-gi$_4$-in-nam]

380. [en-me-er-k]ár du[mu]-^{d}u[tu-ke$_4$] mu-e-ši-in-gi$_4$-in-nam

The herald journeying to Aratta,

350. Heaped up the dust of the journey at his feet,

Pulverized the little stones of the mountains,

Like a dragon *seeking (its) prey* in the plain, he had no rival.

The herald having arrived at Aratta,

The people of Aratta,

Stood admiringly before the *crate*-carrying donkeys;

The herald, in the courtyard of Aratta,

Poured out the grain *for* the storehouse, added ....,

As (if) there were the *rain* of heaven and storm,

Aratta *enjoyed abundance,*

360. Like *gods returning to their dwellings,*

Aratta sated its hunger.

The people of Aratta,

In its water-covered groats ..d the fields.

Afterwards the knights ....,

... the place where water ....,

·· .· · ,

.... ,

... Aratta ....,

To Aratta the word ....,

370. *Obediently* in Aratta *from* the hand ....,

For the lord of Erech, his hand ....:

"We ....,

For the lord of Kullab will *set* carnelian in our ..;

All the elders who are word-wise,

Who together ...., who .. the .. at the wall,

Will *set up* for the lord *that* pure house."

.... ,

[Speaks reverently the word of] his [heart]:

"[Your father my king] has [sent me] to you,

380. [Enmerk]ar the s[on of] U[tu] has sent me to you."

lugal-zu dug₄-ga-ni nam-mu daḫ-[a]-ni [nam]-mu

lugal-mu a-na-b[í-i]n-dug₄ a-na-[bí-in-daḫ-à]m

gidru-mà úr-bi me-n[am]-mun-n[a-k]a

gidru-bi kul-aba^ki-a a [n-dù]l-eš ì-ag

gidru-mul-mul-[la-bi] èš-é-an-na-[k]e₄

kug-^dinanna-ke₄ ní im-ši-ib-te-en-te

gidru um-ta-?-ᴋíᴅ ḫu-mu-u[n-d]a-gál

na₄gug giš-aš   na₄za-gìn giš-as-gim šu-ni-a ḫu-mu-un-gál

en-aratta^ki-ke₄ igi-mu-šè ḫu-mu-un-túm mà-a-ra ḫa-ma-an-dug₄

390. ḫur-gim ḫu-mu-na-ab-bé-a-ka

nam-bi-šè saḫar-a ᴋᴀ ba-an-tu šà-ᴋᴀ-tab-ba ba-an-ná[190]

u₄ im-zal inim im-ᴅùɢ-ᴅùɢ-ᴅùɢ[191]

ᴋᴀ-ᴋᴀ-šè-nu-gar-ra im-me

inim-ma še-anšu-kú-a-gim gìr mi-ni-ib-nigin-e

ì-bí-šè lú lú-ù-ra[192] a-na-na-an-dug₄

lú lú-ra aš a-na-na-an-daḫ

lú lú-ra in-na-ab-be-a ḫur ḫé-en-na-nam-ma-àm

[k]in-gi₄-a lugal-zu en-kul-aba^ki-ra [ù]-na-a-dug₄ ù-na-dè-daḫ[193]

gidru-giš-nam(?)-ᴍᴇ-mu giš na-an-sa₄-sa₄

400. .... šu-na um-ma-ni-in-gar igi um-ši[194]-bar-bar

^gišₐ-am(!) nam-me ^giššim-gig nam-me

^gišerin nam-me ^giššu-úr-me nam-me[195]

^gišḫa-šu-úr [nam-me ^gištaškarin na]m-me

^gišesi nam-me [^giš.. nam-me]

^gišasál-?-^gišgigir-ra nam-me

^giškid-da ^gišꜱᴜḫᴜʀ-na[196] nam-me

guškin nam-me urudu nam-me

kù-me-a-zi-kù-babbar nam-me

na₄gug nam-me   na₄za-gìn nam-me

410. gidru um-ta-?-ᴋíᴅ hu-mu-un-da-gál

na₄gug gis-aš   na₄za-gìn giš-as-gim šu-ni-a hu-mu-un-gál

en-kul-aba^ki-a ke₄ igi-mu-šè ḫu-mu-un-túm[197] e-ne-ra dug₄-mu-na-ab

"Your king, *what* has he spoken, [*what*] has he said?"

"My king, this is what he has spoken, this is what [he has said]:

'My scepter, the base of which is the *me* of princeship,

That scepter has been a pr[otecting sh]ade over Kullab,

[That] all-bright scepter, in the house Eanna,

Of the holy Inanna *has relieved all fear.*

Having .. d the scepter, let him place,

Carnelian (like) *one tree*, lapis lazuli like *one tree*, let him place in his hand,

Let the lord of Aratta bring before me,' he said unto me."

390. After he had thus spoken to him,

He put his mouth to the dust, he lay down in a (ground) hole because of it,

Day broke, he *multiplied words,*

He spoke *confusedly,*

He *circled about in* (*his*) *words* like a donkey eating grain.

What now has man spoken to man?

What has man .. said to man?

What man said to man, it was this:

"O herald, speak to your king, the lord of Kullab, and say unto him:

'My scepter, the ... wood, *it is called wood,*

400. Having placed .... in his hand, having examined it –

It is citrus, it is ..,

It is cedar, it is *cypress,*

It is *juniper*, it is box,

It is *maple*, it is ..,

It is *mulberry*, the .. of the chariot,

It is ....,

It is gold, it is copper,

It is enduring ..-silver, it is silver,

It is carnelian, it is lapis-lazuli,

410. Having .. d the scepter, let him place,

Carnelian (like) *one tree*, lapis-lazuli like *one tree*, let him place in his hand,

Let the lord of Kullab bring it before me,' say unto him."

ḫur-gim ḫu-mu-na-ab-be-a-ka

kin-gi$_4$-a dùr^{úr}-si-?-kud-du-gim ka-si-il-la[198] mu-un-du

anšu-edin-na bar-rím-ma ʀíм-di-gim gìr ì-tag-tag-ge

ᴋᴀ-ɴɪ ɪᴍ-a bi-ib-zi-zi-zi[199]

udu-síg-sù udu-....-du$_7$-du$_7$-gim du$_{10}$-ús-s[a] mu-un-díb

sig$_4$-kul-aba^{ki}-a-ka gìr-ḫúl-la bí-in-gub

lugal-a-ni en-kul-aba^{ki}-a-ra[200]

420. inim-inim-ma mu-na-ra-si-si

en-me-er-kár-ra ^{d}en(?)-ki(?)-ke$_4$ geštug mu-na-a[n-s]ì

en-e izkim-maḫ-a-[ni] á(?) ba-da-a[n-a]g(?)

é-....

lugal-e .... šu ba-ra-an-ti

mu-un-? š[u] bí-.... igi bí-i[n]-?

^{na}$_4$na-ᴋᴀ-ᴋᴀ sim-gim b[a-ni-i]n-ra

^{gi}su-ši-ma ka-zal-gim[201] mu-ni-in-?

u$_4$-ta gissu-šè àm-è-e

gissu-ta u$_4$-šè àm-è-e

430. mu-ía-àm mu-u-àm ba-zal-[la]-ʀɪ[202]

^{gi}su-ši-ma tun-gim bí-in-gaz

en-e igi-ḫúl-la im-ši-in-bar

ɴɪ-ʟɪ-ɴɪ-ɴɪ kur-ᴢᴀ.ᴍùš-a-ka sìg-ga[203] i-ni-in-dé

en-e kin-gi$_4$-a kur-šè du-úr[204]

gidru šu-na mu-un-na-gá-gá

kin-gi$_4$-a aratta^{ki}-aš du-a-ni[205]

?^{mušen}-gim ḫur-sag-gá nim-gim saḫar-nig[in]-a[206]

?^{kua}-gim kur-ùr-ùr-ru ... aratta^{ki}-aš ba-te

kisal-aratta^{ki}-ka gìr-ḫúl-la mi-ni-in-gub[207]

440. ensí-na mu-un-ᴅᴜ

šu-kin si-bí-in-sá-a kin b[í-i]b-ag-e

en-aratta^{ki}-ke$_4$ gidru-ta igi-tab-ba

?-ᴋᴀ ki-tuš-kug-ga-ni-a ɪᴍ-ɪᴍ-kár-kár-ka

en-e šà-tam-a[208]-ni-ir gù mu-na-dé-e

After he had thus spoken to him,

The herald journeyed in the .. like a donkey-foal whose ... is cut off,

Like a donkey of the plain *galloping* on parched land, (his) feet pain;

He lifted *his mouth to the rain*,

Like a *shaggy* sheep, a ... sheep, he *held (on to) a companion*,

In the brickwork of Kullab he set a joyful foot,

To his king, the lord of Kullab,

420. He pours out the words.

Enki granted Enmerkar wisdom;

The lord ..d his lofty omen

The house ....,

The king took ....,

He ..d the .., *examined it*,

Crushed the ..-stone like a herb,

Delightedly *planted* there the ..-reed,

Brought it forth from the light to the shade,

Brought it forth from the shade to the light;

430. After five, after ten years had passed,

He crushed the ..-reed like (*with*) *an axe*;

The lord looked with joyous eye upon it,

In the highland ZA.MÙŠ he *wisely cast his* ..;

The lord, *for* the herald journeying to the land,

Placed the scepter in his hand.

The herald journeying to Aratta,

Like a ..-bird in the mountain, like a fly *in the gath*[*er*]*ed* dust,

Like a ..-fish .... approached Aratta,

In the courtyard of Aratta set a joyous foot,

440. Walked over to his *išakku*,

(*And*) *having attended to the formalities, performs his mission.*

The lord of Aratta, *dazzled* by the scepter,

... in his holy dwelling place ....,

The lord says to his *šatammu*:

aratta^{ki} ganam-sig$_{11}$-gim ḫé-im kaskal-bi [kur-k]i-bala ḫé-im

maḫ-aratta^{ki} kug-^{d}inanna-ke$_{4}$

en-kul-aba^{ki}-ra mu-na-an-sì-ma-ta[209]

lú-kin-gi$_{4}$-a mu-un-gi$_{4}$-a-ni[210]

^{d}utu-è-dè inim-dugud[211] pa-è-dè

450. a-da-al kug-^{d}inanna-ke$_{4}$ igi me-ši-kár-kár[212]

aratta^{ki}-a lul-e me-a[213] ḫé-en-dè-dib-e[214]

al me-da-aš šu al-tag-tag-i-a[215]

me-en-dè sù-ga lul-la-bi-šè

en-kul-aba^{ki}-ra ^{na}$_{4}$gug lul-la-me-a mu-na-dúr-ru-de-en-dè-en[216]

en-aratta^{ki}-ke$_{4}$ kin-gi$_{4}$-a-ar

inim-ma dub-maḫ-gim šu mu-na-an-sì[217]

kin-gi$_{4}$-a lugal-zu en-kul-aba^{ki}-a[218]-ra ù-na-dug$_{4}$ ù-na-dè-daḫ

ur na-an-gig-ge ur na-an-babbar-re[219]

ur na-an-si-e ur na-an-síg(?)-e

460. ur na-an-sig$_{7}$-sig$_{7}$-ge ur na-an-gùn-gùn-gú ur ḫu-mu-ra-ab-sì-mu

ur-mu ur-ra-ni a-da-man ḫé-im-da-e

á-gál ḫé-zu e-ne-ra dug$_{4}$-mu-na-ab

ḫur-gim ḫu-mu-na-ab-bé-a-ka

kin-gi$_{4}$-a ú-lum a-lam mu-un-du

sig$_{4}$-kul-aba^{ki}-ke$_{4}$ egir-sì-ga-gim inim un-gi$_{4}$

?-gim KA-GABA-kur-ra-ka igi mu-ni-ib-íl-íl-i

?-maḫ gír-gír-ta zi-ga-gim é-me-MAN mu-un-ta-lá-lá

en-me-er-kár-dumu ^{d}utu-ke$_{4}$ sag mi-ni-in-íl

. . . . aratta^{ki}-ke$_{4}$ . . . .

470. ki-tuš-a-ni-ta a-maḫ-[è-a-gim mu-un-na-ab]-bé

kin-gi$_{4}$-a en-a[ratt]a^{ki}-ra ù-na-dug$_{4}$ ù-na-dè-daḫ

túg na-an-gig-ge túg na-an-babbar-re

túg na-an-si-e túg na-an-síg-e

túg na-an-sig$_{7}$-sig$_{7}$-ge túg na-an-gùn-gùn-gú túg ḫu-mu-ra-ab-sì-mu

''Aratta-- it(s people) are like scattered ewes, its roads are like inimical

[highland],

The lofty Aratta, since the holy Inanna

Had given it to the lord of Kullab,

The herald whom he has sent,

Who with the rising sun reveals the 'heavy' word,

450. *Lo*, the holy Inanna *looks upon with favor*,

In Aratta, *she walks with him . . . .*,

. . how long will (her) hand smite (us)!

We . . . .,

For the lord of Kullab shall *set* carnelian in our . . .''

The lord of Aratta, to the herald

Entrusted the word like a lofty tablet:

''O herald, speak unto your king, the lord of Kullab, and say unto him:

'A *fighting-man*, not black, a *fighting-man*, not white,

A *fighting-man*, not brown, a *fighting-man*, not . .,

460. A *fighting-man*, not yellow, a *fighting-man*, not dappled; let him give you a *fighting-man*,

Let my *fighting-man* hold a contest with his *fighting-man*,

Let the strong(er) become known,' say unto him.''

After he had thus spoken to him,

The herald journeyed *in all haste*;

Having brought back the word *at* the brickwork of Kullab like a . . .,

He lifts (his) eye like a . . *to* the . . . of the highland,

Stretches out the . . like a . . *rising out of the* . . .

Enmerkar, the son of Utu, raised (his) head,

. . . . of Aratta . . . .,

470. [*Addres*]*sed* him from where he sat [like a migh]ty water-spring:

''O herald, speak unto the lord of A[ratt]a and say unto him:

'A garment, not black, a garment, not white,

A garment, not brown, a garment, not . .,

A garment, not yellow, a garment, not dappled; let him give you a garment;

ur-m[u ur-ig]i-gá [l-la-^{d}en-lí]l-lá ur šu ga-mu-na-šub

ur-mu ur-ra-ni a-da-man ḫé-im-di-e

á-gál ḫé-zu-zu e-ne-ra dug$_4$-mu-na-ab

min-kam-ma-šè ù-na-dug$_4$ ù-na-dè-daḫ

én-tukum-šè lul-da LI-a ḫé-ni-ib-dib-e

480. uru-na udu-gim ... ḫu-mu-un-su$_8$-ub

e-ne sipad-bi-gim egir-bi ḫé-im-uš-e

du-a-ni kur-kù-$^{na}_4$za-gìn-na

gi-níg-dub-ba-gim gú ḫu-mu-na-ab-gar

guškin k[ù-b]abbar sù-du-àm-bi

^{d}inanna nin-é-an-na-ra

kisal-arat[ta^{ki}-a-k]a gur$_7$-šè ḫu-mu-un-dub-dub-bu

eš-kam-ma-[šè] ù-na-dug$_4$ ù-na-dè-daḫ

uru-ni KAS-sag$^{[mušen]}$-gim giš-bi-ta na-an-TAR-ta-ta-an

.... na-an-dúb-bé-en

490. [ki-lam-gál-la-gi]m na-an-si-ig-en

.... líl-e nam-mi-ni-in-dib-bé-en

du-a-ní na$_4$-ḫur-sag-gá šu ù-mu-ni-in-ti

éš-gal-eridu^{ki} ? gán-nun ḫa-ma-dù-e

a-SAL-bar-bi IM-..-ra šu [ḫa-ma-ni]-ib-tag-tag-ge

gissu-bi kal[am-ma] [ḫa-ma]-ni-ib-lá-lá-e

inim-dug$_4$-ga-ni ....-[g]i$_4$-a-ka

izkim-a-ni [e-ne-ra] dug$_4$-mu-na-ab

u$_4$-ba en(?) ....-àm[220]

.... dúr-gar-ra numun-nun-na-ke$_4$-ne

500. ... DIŠ-a-mú-a

dug$_4$-ga-ni ..-àm šà-bi su-su-a-àm

kin-gi$_4$-a KA NI-dugud šu nu-mu-un-da-an-gi$_4$-gi$_4$

kin-gi$_4$-a KA NI-dugud šu nu-mu-un-da-an-gi$_4$-gi$_4$-da-ka[221]

en-kul-aba^{ki}-a-ke$_4$ im-e šu bi-in-ra inim dub-gim b[í-i]n-gub

u$_4$-bi-ta KA im-ma-gub-bu nu-ub-ta-gál-la

M[y] fighting-man, the *champion* of [Enli]l, the fighting-man I will *set loose against* him,

My fighting-man will hold a contest with his fighting-man,

The strong(er) will become known,' say unto him.

A second time speak unto him and say unto him:

'*How long will he walk deceitfully in* ..?

480. In his city let the .. *walk* like sheep,

Let him follow behind them like their shepherd,

When he comes, the highland of silver and lapis-lazuli,

Having prostrated itself before him like *heaped up* reeds,

Its gold, s[ilv]er, (and) *precious stones*,

For Inanna, the queen of Eanna,

Let him heap up in the courtyard of Arat[ta] *for* the storehouse.'

A third time speak unto him and say unto him:

'I will make (the people of) his city *flee* like the ..-bird from its tree,

I will crush the ....,

490. I will make it *desolate* like a place of ...,

I will make walk in it the ....,

When he comes, having taken the stones of the mountains,

Let him build for me the *ganunnu*, the great shrine *of* Eridu,

Embellish [for me] its ....,

Spread its shade [for me] [over the la]nd,

After he had .... his uttered word,

His omen,' say unto him.''

Then the lord ....,

.... *the dwelling of the princely seed*,

500. *Rising* ....,

His command is .., *its* ''heart'' is *obscure*,

The herald *was heavy of mouth, could not repeat it*,

Because the herald *was heavy of mouth, could not repeat it*,

The lord of Kullab *patted (a lump of) clay, set up the words* like a tablet —

Formerly there had been no one who *set words on clay* —

i-bí-šè ^{d}utu u$_4$-NE-a ḫur ḫé-en-nam-ma-àm

en-kul-aba^{ki}-a-ke$_4$ in[im dub-gim b]í-in-gub ḫur h[é-en]-nam-ma[222]

kin-gi$_4$-a mušen-gim á-dúb ì-ag-e

ur-bar-ra maš-e-ús-sa-gim guru$_5$-uš ì-búr-búr-re

510. ḫur-sag-ía ḫur-sag-àš ḫur-sag-imin im-me-ri-bal-bal

igi mu-un-íl aratta^{ki}-aš ba-te

kisal-aratta^{ki}-ka gìr-ḫúl-la mi-ni-in-gub

nam-nir-gál-lugal-a-na mu-un-zu

búr-ra-bi inim-šà-ga-na bi-íb-bé

kin-gi$_4$-a en-ar[at]ta^{ki}-ra mu-na-ab-bal-e

a-a-zu lugal-[mu] mu-e-ši-in-gi$_4$-in-nam

en-unu^{ki}-g[a e]n-kul-aba^{ki}-a-ke$_4$ mu-[e-si]-in-gi$_4$-in-nam

lugal-zu du[g$_4$-ga-ni] nam-mu daḫ-a-ni nam-mu

lugal-mu [a-na bí-i]n-dug$_4$ a-na bí-in-daḫ-àm[223]

520. lugal-mu .... dumu-^{d}en-líl-lá-ke$_4$[224]

.... da-mú-a

.... ús-sa-àm

.... gub-ba-bi

nam-en nam-lugal-la pa-è-ag-a[225]

en-me-er-kár-dumu-^{d}utu-ke$_4$ im ma-an-sì

en-aratta^{ki}-ke$_4$ im igi ù-ni-bar[226] šà-inim-ma ù-bí-zu[227]

a-[n]a-ma-ab-bé-en-na-bi ù-mu-e-dug$_4$

a-ru-a su$_6$-^{na_4}za-gìn-sù(?)-da-ar[228]

áb-kalag-ga-ni kur-me-sikil-la KA-kéš-da-ar

530. [sa]ḫar-unu^{ki}-ga-ka á-è-a-ar

amaš-áb-zi-da-ka ga-kú-a-ar

kul-aba^{ki} kur-me-gal-gal-la-ka nam-en-na-du-ma-ar[229]

en-me-er-kár-dumu-^{d}utu-ra

inim-bi èš-é-an-na-ka inim-dùg ga-mu-na-ab-dug$_4$[230]

gi$_6$-pàr ^{giš}teḫi-gibil-gim gurun-íl-la-na

lugal-mu en-kul-aba^{ki}-ra šu-a ga-mu-na-ab-gi$_4$

ḫur-gim ḫu-mu-na-ab-bé-a-ka[231]

Now *as* Utu *is* . . . , it was so,

The lord of Kullab *set up words* like a tablet — it was so.

The herald flaps (his) wings,

Like a wolf following a kid, he *loosens* (his) . . .

510. Five mountains, six mountains, seven mountains he crossed,

Lifted (his) face, approached Aratta,

In the courtyard of Aratta he set a joyous foot,

Made known the exaltedness of his king,

Speaks reverently the word of his heart.

The herald says to the lord of Ar[at]ta:

"Your father, [my] king, has sent me to you,

The lord of Erech, the lord of Kullab, has sent me [to you]."

"Your king, what has [he sp]oken, what has he said?"

"My king, this is [*what*] he has spoken, this is what he has said —

520. My king, ... , the son of Enlil,

. . . . *rising* . . . . ,

. . . . *adjacent to* . . . . ,

. . . . its . . . . ,

Who makes manifest lordship and kingship—

Enmerkar, the son of Utu, has given me a clay (tablet),

O lord of Aratta, examine the clay (tablet), learn the 'heart' of (his) word;

Command what I shall say concerning this matter,

(And) to the dedicated one who *wears a long* beard of lapis lazuli,

To him whose mighty cow . . s the land of pure divine decrees,

530. To him whose seed came forth in the dust of Erech,

To him who was fed milk in the fold of the faithful cow,

To him who was fit for the lordship *over* Kullab, the land of all the great *me*,

To Enmerkar, the son of Utu,

I will speak that word as a good word in the temple of Eanna;

In the *giparru* which bears fruit like a fresh . . .-plant,

I will deliver it to my king, the lord of Kullab."

After he had thus spoken to him,

en-aratta^{ki}-ke$_4$ kin-gi$_4$-a [232]

im-šu-RIN-na-ni šu ba-ši-in-ti

540. en-aratta^{ki}-ke$_4$ im-ma igi i-ni-in-bar [233]

inim-dug$_4$-ga KAK-àm sag-ki MI-rí-da-àm

en-aratta^{ki}-ke$_4$ im-šu-RIN-na-ni igi im-bar-bar-re

u$_4$-ba en-men[234]-nam-en-na-du-ma dumu-^{d}en-líl-lá-ke$_4$

^{d}iškur an-ki-a gù-nun-bi di-dam

u$_4$-du$_7$-du$_7$ UG-gal ....-ka nam-mi-ni-in-gub

kur-kur .... mu-un-tuk$_4$-tuk$_4$-e

ḫur-sag .... mu-un-da-ḫa-ḫa-e

ní-me-lám(?) .... gaba-na-gál-la-bi

ḫur-sag(?)-ka-zal-la sag mi-ni-in-íl

550. aratta^{ki} bar-u$_4$-bi šà-ḫur-sag-gá-ka

gig ní-bi-mú-a gú ní-bi an-ga-mú-a

gig ní-bi-mú-a gur$_7$ ..-KA

en-aratta^{ki}-ra mu-na-in-tu-[tu]

kisal-aratta^{ki}-a-ka igi-ni-šè i-im-dub(?) [235]

en-aratta^{ki}-ke$_4$ gig-e igi bi-in-du$_8$

kin-gi$_4$-a igi-ugula-ugula-a-ni mu-un-ši-ib-?-?-e [236]

en-aratta^{ki}-ke$_4$ kin-gi-a-ar gù mu-na-dé-e

maḫ-bi ^{d}inanna nin-kur-kur-ra-ke$_4$

é(?)-ni aratta^{ki} šu li-bí-in-dag [237] unu^{ki}-e la-ba-an-dug$_4$

560. é-za-gìn-na-ka-ni šu li-bí-in-dag ès-e-an-na-ka la-ba-an-dug$_4$

kur-me-sikil-la-ka šu li-bí-in-dag sig$_4$-kul-aba^{ki}-a-ke$_4$ [238] la-ba-an-dug$_4$

^{giš}ná-še-ir-kán-ka šu li-bí-in-dag ^{giš}ná-gi-rin-na la-[239]-ba-an-dug$_4$

en-ra šu-sikil-la-ka-ni šu li-bí-in-dag en-unu^{ki}-ra [240] en-kul-aba^{ki}-a-ra

    la-ba-an-dug$_4$ [241]

aratta^{ki} zi-da-gùb-bu-ba [242]

^{d}inanna nin-kur-kur-ra-ke$_4$

a-maḫ-è-a-gim mu-un-na-nigin

The lord of Aratta, from the herald

Took his *oven*—

540. The lord of Aratta examined the clay (tablet),

The commanded word is *nail-like*, the appearance is ... —

The lord of Aratta examines his *oven*.

Then did the lord fit for the crown of lordship, the son of Enlil,

Ishkur, the thunderer of heaven and earth,

The attacking storm, the great *lion step up in* .. ,

Makes all the lands .... tremble,

Makes the mountains .... *quake*,

With fear (and) *terror* .... *on his breast*,

He lifted (his) head *on the mountain of delight*,

550. Into Aratta whose *white* (*wall*) *face* is the heart of the mountain,

Wheat growing of itself, *beans* also growing of themselves,

Wheat growing of itself, into the .. storehouse,

He brings before the lord of Aratta,

In the courtyard of Aratta he *heaped up* before him.

(When) the lord of Aratta saw the wheat,

He *invites* the herald before his *supervisors*,

The lord of Aratta says to the herald:

"Its lofty (one), Inanna, the queen of all the lands,

Has not *abandoned* her *house* Aratta, has not *handed it over to* Erech,

560. Has not *abandoned* her lapis-lazuli house, has not *handed it over to* the

shrine Eanna,

Has not *abandoned* the highland of the pure *me*, has not *handed it over to*

the brickwork of Kullab,

Has not *abandoned* the *adorned* bed, has not *handed it over to* the *fruitful* bed,

Has not *abandoned* her pure *hand for* the lord, has not *handed it over to* the

lord of Kullab."

Aratta, right and left

Did Inanna, the queen of all the lands,

Like a mighty (water-) spring *surround for him*,

lú-bi-ne lú lú-ta-dar-a

lú ^{d}dumu-zi-dè lú-ta è-me-eš

inim-kù-^{d}inanna ki-bi-šè gar-gar-me-eš

570. ur-igi-gál-la ?-a-sARr^{d}dumu-zi-da ḫé-ši-im-?

. . . .

. .-a-ma-ru-ka gub-ba-me-eš

á-a-ma-ru ba-ùr-ra-ta

^{d}inanna nin-kur-kur-ra-ke$_{4}$

nam-gal-ki-ág-^{d}dumu-zi-da-ke$_{4}$

a-nam-ti-la-ka mu-un-ne-sù-sù

gú-kalam-ma-ka giš(?) mu-un-ne-en-gál

ur-igi-gál-la du-a-ni

^{túg}sag-šu-dar-a ugu-na i-im-šú

580. túg-UG-ÚG-gá^{243} zag mu-ni-in-kéš

. .-íl-la . . . . mi-ni-in-du$_{8}$-[du$_{8}$]

. . . . TE-na mi-ni-in-[d]ug$_{4}$

. . . . nin . . . ba-an-sìg^{244}

. . . .-a-ni

. . . . ^{d}inanna

LI.DU-ni ^{d}ama-uš [umgal-an-na] . . .-a-na ba-dùg

u$_{4}$-bi-ta PI-kug PI . . . . .-^{d}dumu-zi-da-ke$_{4}$

šu mu-ni-in-du$_{7}$ EZEN mu-[ni-in]-. . inim mu-ni-in-zu

um-ma kur-me-sikil-šè du-a-ni

590. ki sikil u$_{4}$-da-na-til-la-gim im-ma-na-ta-è

šim-zi-da igi-na mu-un-dar

. .-babbar-ra zag mu-ni-in-kèš

. .-zi-da u$_{4}$-^{d}nanna-gim mu-un-è

. . . . sag si mu-un-sá

. . .-a-ni en-me-er-kár bara-gi$_{4}$ mu-un-da-ab-si

. . . . um-mi-in-zi-zi^{245}

. . [im]-da-LU-LU aratta^{ki}-aš ganam-da sila$_{4}$-bi

. . [im]-da-LU-LU aratta^{ki}-aš uz-da máš-bi

Its men, men who were .. *out of* men,

Men whom Dumuzi *had brought forth out of men,*

Who set the words of Inanna in their place,

570. *Whom* the *champion* ... of Dumuzi did ..,

....,

Who *stood in* the .. of the flood —

After the violence of the flood had raged,

Inanna, the queen of all the lands,

Because she greatly loved Dumuzi,

Sprinkled the water of life for them,

Produced trees for them *everywhere* in the land.

The champion, *when* he *came,*

Was covered with a ..-helmet,

580. Was arrayed in lion (-skin) garments,

..d in ....,

..d in ....,

Smote ... the queen ....,

His ....,

Inanna ....,

His songs *pleased* Amaushumgalanna ....,

The holy *rites of* former days, the .... *rites* of Dumuzi,

He perfected, [*established*] feasts, made known the word.

The ''old woman'', *when she came* to the land of the pure *me,*

590. *Brought out the maid to him before the end of day,*

Painted her eyes with kohl,

Arrayed herself in a white [*garment*],

Brought forth the ... like the light of Nanna,

Directed the .....

His ..., Enmerkar *filled the* .. *crate,*

Having raised up ....,

The .. *walk together to* Aratta, with the ewe its lamb,

The .. *walk together to* Aratta, with the goat its kid,

.. [im]-da-LU-LU aratta^{ki}-aš áb-da amar-bi

600. .. [i]m-da-LU-LU aratta^{ki}-aš ? dùr^{úr}-?-gig-ga

.. [ar]atta^{ki}-a na-an-da-bé-a

.. [ḫé]-im-dub-dub gú ḫé-im-gar-gar

....-za-a ḫé-gál-zu

.... en-aratta^{ki}-ra ù-mu-ni-in-ag

....-ra ḫé-en-..

.... mu-un-di-ni-ib-..-e

.... mu-un-ta-è

.... si mu-un-na-ab-sá

....

610. ....

....

.... me-te .... [-gá]l

... SI i-lu-šà- ....

...-a ḫé-gál-zu AN ....

... ^{d}en-líl-le sag-eš mu-ré-in-rig$_{7}$ .. la-šè(?) ḫé-zu-zu

[en-me-er]-kar a-a-ni nu-lam-lam a nu-un-dé

^{d}en-l[íl-lugal-kur]-kur-ra-ke$_{4}$ ḫu-mu-kár-re IM-ba

éš-kar .. [i]m-ma-an-dù-a-gim

nam-lú-lu$_{6}$^{lu}-aratta^{ki}-ke$_{4}$

620. guškin kù $^{na_{4}}$za-gìn bal-ag-dè éš-kàr-...

lú-gurun-guškin gurun giš gub-bu-ne

^{giš}ma geštin-ba níg-...-ba-gim gur$_{7}$-gal-š[è] ù(?)-mu-un-dub

$^{na_{4}}$za-gìn-a úr-ba mu-un-búr-re-ne

^{gi}ušub pa-ba mu-un-...-e-ne

^{d}inanna nin-e-an-na-ra

kisal-é-an-na-ka gur$_{7}$-šè mu-un-dub-bu-ne

lugal-mu gá-nu na ga-e-ri na-ri-mu ḫé-e-díb

inim ga-ra-ab-dug$_{4}$ gizzal ḫé-[bí]-ag

... šim-kur-kur-ra kalam-e ù-um-pàd

630. .... aratta^{ki} ....

The .. *walk together to* Aratta, with the cow its calf,

600. *.. walk together to Aratta* .. the donkey-foal ....,

.. in Aratta *speaks* with him:

"Heap up .., submit,

In your ...., your overflow,

Make .... for the lord of Aratta,

Let him ....,

He will ....,

He has brought forth ....,

He directed for him ....,

....,

610. ....,

....,

.... the (vital) need ....,

.... *wail* ....,

.... your abundance ....,

... Enlil has presented to you as a gift, ... *make known,*

[Enmer]kar, his father, has not ..d, has not poured water,

Enlil, the king of all the lands will ....."

Like a .. task which is done,

The people of Aratta,

620. To *transport* gold, silver, (and) lapis-lazuli, *the task* ...,

The men who set up gold "fruit," as "tree-fruit,"

Having heaped it in its fig (and) vine like ... *for* the large storehouse,

Cover their *roots* with lapis lazuli,

.. the reed .. on *their branches,*

For Inanna, the queen of Eanna,

In the courtyard of Eanna they heap them up *for* the storehouse.

"Come, my king, instruction I would offer you, take my instruction,

A word I would speak to you, give ear to it:

Choose the ... *herbs* of all the lands, *for* the land,

630. .... Aratta ....,

.. me-šè i-im-da-HE IM-me-NE

[m]à-e gú-e-ta du-a-mu-de

?-mu nin-mul-mul-e ma-an-sì

^dgeštin-[an-na] . . . .

uru-ba LÍL . . . .

EZEN nu-mu-. . . .

u₄-šú-uš nam-. . . .

. . . . ,

I, when I come from the . . . ,

The *shining* queen gave me my . . ,

Geshtinanna . . . . ,

In their city . . . . ,

The feast . . . . ,

Daily . . . . .

COMMENTARY

Lines 1-32. These lines contain a preamble or introduction and are not part of the story; a similar preamble begins the epic tale "Enmerkar and Ensukushiranna," lines 1-13. For *gaba-u₄-da* (line 2), cf. e.g., *AS* 12:28, line 112. For rendering of *kur* (line 3), cf. *BASOR* 96:24, note 24. For *še-gu-nu-* (line 9), cf. now Landsberger, *JNES* 8:281 ff. For the land Dilmun (line 11) and its possible location, cf. *BASOR* 96:18 ff. For the *giparru* in connection with the *ènu*, cf. e.g., *AS* 12:60, line 349. For *bala—ag*, cf. line 620.

Lines 33-64. Perhaps *kur-*ZA.MÙŠ*-* (line 34) is to be read *šuba*, (cf. *ŠL* 586:41,42). For Enmerkar (line 35), cf. Jacobsen *AS* 11:86, note 115. The rendering of *sù-du-ám* (line 41) by "precious stone" is a guess based on the context. According to line 43, Erech had an Inanna temple known as *é-anšanna*, just as Ur had an Inanna temple known as *é-dilmunna*. The *èš-gal* and the *unú-gal* mentioned in lines 51 and 52 cannot be identified more closely. For *me* (line 53), cf. now the references listed in *JCS* 5:15.

Lines 65-104. The implications of line 66 are not too clear. For *in-nin₇*, cf. line 223, where a meaning such as "mistress" seems to suit the context; cf., however, Falkenstein, *ZA* 49:126. In line 72, the last sign might perhaps preferably be read *-tumu*, since the verb should probably be a present-future rather than a preterit. The implications of lines 75-76 are not clear. In line 76, the last sign might perhaps preferably be read *-gala*, since the verb should probably be a present-future. The rendering of *-lu-a* in line 77 is a guess only; the reading *lu* seems preferable to *dib* since *dib-a* would probably be written *dib-ba*. Instead of *ma-gá-gá* (line 79), one might have expected *ḫa-ra-gá-gá*. In line 94 note the fuller writing *-e-e* in the verbal form (cf. line 63). The rendering of line 100 is far from certain; it follows Jacobsen's interpretation of several similar passages in *JNES* 2:119 ff. It assumes that *-šà-* is for *-šà-ga-*, and that *šu-dug₄-ga* is to be understood. So rendered, the line would consist of two epithets descriptive of the lord of Aratta, who would be the subject of the verb in the line following. A more obvious rendering of the line might be "the mighty water of the fields of Dumuzi," but this would hardly fit the context. In line 101, note that instead of *-gar* one might have expected *-gá-gá*. In line 102, the rendering of the first complex is of course uncertain, and in any case its implications are obscure.

Lines 105-160. For lines 106-113, cf. lines 71-78. In line 113, note that *-nigin-e* seems to be for *-nigin-en*. For *ù-na-dug₄* and *ù-na-dè-daḫ* (line 114), cf. Falkenstein *ZA* 44:11 ff. For the prefix in line 115 and following, cf. Falkenstein *ZA* 47:181 ff. The rendering and true meaning of lines 121-123 are very doubtful. In line 124 *a-* seems to be for *ù* in *a-ba-ni-in-ag*, perhaps influenced by a final *-a* of the preceding complex (broken in our case, cf. line 284). For *kug-me-a* (line 125), cf. Falkenstein *ZA* 48:88. The rendering of *bara* with "crates" is a guess only, since "dais" hardly seems to fit (cf. lines 282 and 283, where *bara* seems to be parallel to *sa-al-kad₅-e*). If the rendering of lines 128-130 is correct, the variant in note 51 must be a scribal error. The rendering "light" for *si muš—dar-dar* (line 132) is a guess only; so too is "adorn" for *šеš—mul-* (line 133). For the "golden age" passage, cf. Jacobsen, *JNES* 5:148 and *JAOS* 68:7, note 47.

Lines 161-218. Line 164 seems to be a variant of lines 72 and 107 (cf. note 20 and perhaps note 64). In line 179, the rendering "what" for *nam-mu* is a guess only, cf. Falkenstein, *ZA* 44:15. The implications of line 185 are not clear since neither the "cow" nor the "highland" can be identified, cf. also lines 211 and 213. Note that following 209, the "golden age" passage is omitted. For line 210, cf. Falkenstein, *ZA* 44:7 ff. In line 212, *-aratta^{ki}-* seems to be an error for *-unu^{ki}-*, cf. line 530; note that the first sign should perhaps be read *iš* and be rendered by "mountain."

Lines 219-227. The word *giš* in line 222 is difficult to interpret; "tree" hardly seems to fit. For *in-nin₇*, cf. comment to line 66. For line 225, cf. *SEM* 1 obv. ii 40.

Lines 228-237. In line 233, if the plural form of the verb is not an error, the subject is perhaps to be understood as Enmerkar and the people of Erech. In line 237, note the omission of the subject element; also the seemingly preterit verbal form (cf., however, comment to line 76).

49

Lines 238-294.   For *giš-bur-* (line 245), cf. now Falkenstein, *ZA* 49:322. For *ḫu-ri-in-* (line 246), cf. *ŠL* 78:19 and e.g., *SEM* 1 obv. i 29. In line 255 *adaman* may also be rendered "disputation," "debate," cf. now *BASOR* 122:30; in our poem it seems to stand for the single combat between two "champions," cf. line 458 ff. Lines 256-259 seem to be a proverb; perhaps the implication is that those who are practiced in the contest or debate are victorious and can take the measure of their opponent. In line 264, note the thematic particle *ša-* of the first verbal form, also the preterit with *ḫé-* (cf. *JCS* 1:34). In lines 265 and 266, the "lion" and "ox" refer perhaps to Enmerkar. The meaning of 269-281 is obscure, the attempted rendering merely ascribes the more usual meanings to the individual words and phrases, and is highly uncertain. Lines 269-274, according to this rendering, are a highly poetic description of the *kur-me-sikil-la-* of line 276; in line 270 the first complex might be transliterated as *an-usan-na*; line 271 refers presumably to the setting sun.   The identity of the individual referred to in line 275 is uncertain, and consequently the acts described in lines 276-281 cannot be fitted into the context; the translation of lines 279-281, in particular, is most doubtful. For *mu-un-*TAR in line 281, cf. *AS* 12:48, line 270, but it is difficult to relate it to the preceding *erin-na*. With line 282 ff. the context becomes clear; the lord of Aratta is ready to yield (lines 292-294) if and when Enmerkar brings him large quantities of grain and heaps them up in the courtyard of Aratta, particularly since the goddess Inanna has turned against him. For *a-ba-an-sì* (line 284), cf. comment to line 124. In line 285, the rendering of *gur₇-šè* is uncertain. The translation of the first two complexes in line 286 which treats them as a parallel of the series of two-complex sets which follow is of course a guess only; for a different view, cf. Jacobsen, *BASOR* 102:13 ff. The implications of line 288 are not clear. In line 292 note the thematic particle *ša-* in the verbal form, cf. line 264; and in line 293, note the thematic particle *ši-*. In line 294, the reading of the fourth sign as *tur* rather than as *dumu* (cf. Falkenstein, *ZA* 48:86) is of course an assumption only.

Lines 295-308.   For the rendering of the *ka-zal-gim* (lines 297 and 303) as an adverbial phrase, cf. *JCS* 1:37. For SUN- (line 298), cf. Falkenstein, *ZA* 47:212; for *ḫaš-*, cf. *SS* 1:30. For *-gú-en-na-* (line 301), cf. e.g., "Inanna's Descent," line 35, where it is an assembly shrine or hall of the gods. The rendering of line 305 is uncertain. The meaning of line 306 is not too clear.

Lines 309-347.   The implications of lines 309-310, if the translation is correct, are not too clear; perhaps they intend to reveal Enmerkar's preoccupation with the lord of Aratta's message and the steps to be taken by him as a consequence. The purpose of the acts described in lines 311-317 is not clear. For *-i-gi₈-* (lines 315 and 318) as a variant writing of *igi*, cf. Falkenstein, *ZA* 48:78. Lines 319-321 seem to contain epithets of the goddess Nidaba whose "wisdom-house" (line 322) is also known probably as "Anu's palace" (line 323; Anu is Nidaba's father); he enters for purposes of advice and instruction. According to line 324, it seems that the *lidga* (the rendering "silo" is a guess only) was situated in the *ganunnu*. Lines 327-330 are full of difficulties; the translation is of course highly tentative. In line 332, the verbal form is rendered as if it read *a-ba-an-sì*, cf. comment to line 284. "The people" in line 336 seems to refer to those Erechites who accompany the herald as a grain-carrying caravan, but, if so, the comparison with "ants in their hole" does not seem apt. In line 342, a more literal rendering of the last two complexes might be "has been made into a protecting shade." Lines 343-344 might perhaps be rendered: "(Because of) that all-bright scepter, in the shrine Eanna, the holy Inanna has banished all fear." For the seemingly preterit *ḫu-mu-un-gál* (line 345), cf. comment to line 75. The reading and meaning of *giš-aš* in line 346 are uncertain. For the seemingly preterit *ḫu-mu-un-túm* (line 347), cf. comment to line 72.

Lines 348-377.   In line 351 the translation "pulverized" is a guess based on the context. The renderings of line 358 ff. are of course highly tentative; but the translation of the crucial line 381 seems reasonably certain. Line 359 might perhaps be literally rendered, "Aratta was made into abundance"; the meaning "abundance" rather than "overflow" (i.e., "inundation") seems to be preferable here since the line seems to parallel line 361. For *rá-gaba*, "knight," cf. now, e.g., "Inanna's Descent," line 299. The crucial lines 373-374 are unfortunately very difficult, cf. lines 453-454, the last two lines of the lord of Aratta's address to his *šatammu*. In line 376, "*that* pure house" should refer to Eridu-Apsû (cf. lines 54-55).

Lines 378-389.   Line 378 should in some way refer to the herald. For lines 379-382, cf. lines 177-180. In line 387, the fourth sign is not -AN- (cf. lines 345 and 410).

Lines 390-412.   Lines 391-394 refer presumably to the lord of Aratta. Lines 395-397 are introduced by the poet as a stylistic device to heighten suspense; difficult is the seemingly inexplicable *aš* in line 396. For lines 411-412, cf. lines 345-346.

Lines 413-435.   Lines 414-420 describe the herald's return to Aratta; in line 417, the meaning of the last two complexes, if correctly translated, is not clear (it should refer in some way to the difficulty of the journey). For the final -RI in line 430, cf. perhaps *AS* 12:96. For the rendering *sìg-ga* (line 433), cf. perhaps note 203.

Lines 436-462. The translation of line 440 is most uncertain. For *šu-kin* (line 441), cf. now *JAOS* 69:18. The rendering "dazzled" for *igi-tab-ba* (line 442) is of course a guess only. In line 443 note the very strange final complex. The translation of lines 450-454 is highly doubtful; for *a-da-al* (line 450), cf. *AS* 12:92; for lines 453-454, cf. lines 372-373. In line 456, the *-ma* of *inim-ma* seems unjustified; the implications of "like a lofty tablet" are not quite clear. The crucial word in the passage contained in line 458 ff. is of course *ur*; the rendering "fighting-man" rather than "dog," "servant," "beast," etc., seems to suit the context. The colors listed in lines 458-460 are those found in the syllabaries except for that denoted by the final complex in line 459.

Lines 463-497. In line 464 the rendering of *ú-lum a-lam* by "in all haste" is a guess only. For *a-maḫ-è-a-* (line 470), cf. Falkenstein, *ZA* 49:322. Lines 472-474 are identical with 458-460 except for the substitution of *túg* for *ur*; lines 476-477 are practically identical with lines 461-462. In line 480 the broken complex should refer to Aratta's people or the like. To judge from lines 482-484 (unless these are highly poetic in character), (the people) of "the highland of silver and lapis-lazuli" were vassals of Aratta. Lines 488-491 contain Enmerkar's threat of destruction to Aratta, which differs considerably from that contained in lines 115-120. The translation and implications of lines 496-497 are uncertain.

Lines 498-507. The translation and interpretation of this passage are quite uncertain. In lines 502-503, the translation assumes that signs 4-6 are to be read *ka i-dugud*; the translation "repeat" instead of "deliver" for *šu—gi₄* is a guess based on the context. Line 506 seems to be an oath-like expression used by the Sumerian poet for heightening the effect of his statement, cf. *SS* 1:12 (line 52), where the same explanation no doubt holds.

Lines 508-536. For lines 510-519, cf. lines 171-180. Lines 520-524 must have contained epithets of Enmerkar (the first complex in line 521 is probably to be restored as *lugal-mu*), cf. line 181 ff. For lines 527-536, cf. lines 209-219 (note that line 530 has here the correct *unu^{ki}* instead of *aratta^{ki}*.

Lines 537-564. The well-known rendering "oven" for *im-šu-RIN-na-* (lines 539 and 542) is difficult; a meaning such as "oven(-baked)-tablet" for the complex would of course suit the context much better. Line 541 seems to describe the appearance of the written signs; on the other hand, it may perhaps describe in some way the lord of Aratta's despondency upon reading its contents. Lines 542-555, if the translation is correct, describe Ishkur's intervention on the lord of Aratta's behalf for some unstated reason. In line 549 *ḫur-sag-ka-zal-la*, if the reading of the second sign is correct, probably refers to the mountain on which Aratta is located. In line 555, note the correct use of the locative governed by *igi—du₈*. The meaning "abandon" or the like for *šu—dag* (line 559 ff.; cf., however, note 237) is reasonably certain, cf. *SEM* pl. 6, 16-17; the difficulty is with the final verb which the translation assumes to be *šu—dug₄* rather than *-dug₄*, that is, the scribe presumably intended the *šu* of *šu—dag* to be understood as applying also to the second verbal form (cf. notes 239 and 241 for variants which have *šu—dug₄* but strangely enough seem to omit the negative particle *la-* demanded by the sense). Both verbs *šu—dag* and *šu—dug₄* govern the locative *-e* (in the texts of our period *-a* as well). In line 562 "the *adorned* bed" was in Aratta, while "the *fruitful* bed" was in Erech; note too that the second complex but one might have been expected to read *^{giš}ná-gi-rin-na-ka*. Line 563, if the *šu* of the second complex means "hand," the meaning is difficult to follow: the first *en-ra* is troublesome, so too is the *-ka-* of the second complex.

Lines 565-end. From here on the context is difficult to follow, cf. the Introduction. The nature and purpose of Inanna's action (lines 565-567) is not clear. Lines 567-572 seem to describe the men of Aratta, except that line 570 seems to contain a finite verb instead of a participle; note too in this line *ur-igi-gál-la*, cf. perhaps lines 475 and 578. The translation of line 577 is highly doubtful, particularly the words *gú* and *giš(?)*; note too that *-kalam-ma-* is probably not to be taken here to refer to Sumer. The *um-ma* of line 589 and the *ki-sikil* of line 590 cannot be identified more closely in the broken context. Just how Enmerkar fits into the context in line 595 is of course uncertain; for *bara-gi₄*, cf. now Falkenstein, *ZA* 49:126. In lines 597-600, the verbal form may precede the nominal complexes for poetic effect. Line 601 seems to introduce a speech. In line 617 note the final IM-*ba* following the verbal form. Lines 618-626 show with reasonable certainty that the people of Aratta did bring Enmerkar the gold, silver, and lapis lazuli he had demanded, although much of the passage is obscure. Lines 627-628 introduce a speech consisting of words of advice (probably) to Enmerkar; the identity of the speaker who addresses Enmerkar with the words "my king" is uncertain; perhaps it is the herald.

1. B omits *-e*.   2. B omits *-e*.
3. B: *lagab-^{na}₄za-gìn-na*.   4. B: *-ba*.
5. So B; in A the verb begins with *nu-um-*. Note, too, that the reading *-e₁₁-* rather than *-è-* is not quite certain.
6. In C these two lines seem to be written as three lines, but their fragmentary text is difficult to reconcile with the text of A; the lines read: .... [*é*]-*an-na-gim*, ...-^{d}*inanna-ra*, and .... *mu-un-na-dù*. In D the line which should correspond to line 32 begins with *sig₄*; perhaps, therefore, the line begins with *sig₄-*[*kul-aba^{ki}*], which seems to correspond more to line 31.
7. D probably omits *-za-*.   8. D has *nin-* for *nin₇-*.   9. D adds *-ir*.   10. D: *nin-* for *nin₇-*.   11. So D; A omits *-^{d}inanna* and reads *aratta^{ki}* probably before *unu^{ki}-šè* which is destroyed.   12. E: *-ra-* for *-ma-*.   13. E: *-ra-* for *-ma-*.
14. E according to the original reads: [*unu^{ki} kul*]-*aba^{ki} sag-men-kug-gál-la-mu-dè*.
15. E omits *-un-*.   16. E omits *-un-*.
17. E omits *-ge-*.   18. E omits *-un-*.
19. In E the verb probably reads: *ḫu-mu-ši-bar-bar-re*.   20. F has *-gi-* instead of *-gal-zu-*, cf. lines 107 and 164.
21. E omits *ḫé-*.   22. F reads *alan-bi* for *ḫur-sag-alan-ta*; E probably has *-šè* for *-ta*.
23. E omits *ḫé-*.   24. In F the sign following *dar-* does not seem to be identical with that in A; F also omits the following *-ki-* altogether.   25. F: *nar(!?)-*.
26. C inserts *-gi-* before *-gim*.   27. In E the verb seems to read [*ḫu-m*]*u-ra-a*[*n*]-*gál*.
28. C inserts *-un-*.   29. E: *-ib-*.
30. The reading is according to line 61; in C, the only text preserved at this point, there seems to be a variant reading for the first two signs.
31. Between lines 106 and 107, G inserts a line which reads: .. [*k*]*ug kin-gi₄-a-ni* .....
32. G: *má-e* for *me-a*.   33. In G, *ḫu-* precedes *mu-*.   34. G inserts *-gi-* before *-gim*.
35. So G; A omits *-e*.   36. G: *-ke₄* for *-ra*.
37. G inserts *-a-*.   38. G: *-ne-* for *-na-*.
39. In G this line is written as two lines.
40. G: *-ni* for *-bi*.   41. G omits *-sag-*.

42. H: *nam-?-dal-le-en*.   43. H perhaps: *n*[*am-bi-ib-*]*-?-en*.   44. H (and probably D and G): *nam-si-si-ge*.   45. D: *-la-*.
46. H: *nam-ḫa-za-e*.   47. So H; A: *-en* for *-e*.
48. H: *-gi* for *-gi₄*.   49. E omits *-a-*.
50. In E *-e-* follows *-mud-*.   51. E: *-šè* for *-la-ke₄*.   52. C: *-an-ur-* for *-gan-nun-*.
53. E: *-bi*.   54. E: *-kam* for *-ke₄*.
55. C inserts *-la-* before *-àm*; E: *-la* for *-àm*.
56. C inserts *-la-* before *-àm*; E: *-la* for *-àm*. In C lines 136-138 are written as two lines.
57. C inserts *-la-* before *-àm*; E: *-la* for *-àm*.
58. C inserts *-la-* before *-àm*; E: *-la* for *-àm*.
59. C inserts *-la-* before *-àm*.   60. C adds *-àm*.   61. C: *ki-ḫe-me-zi* for [*ki-ḫa*]*-ma-zi^{ki}*.   62. I: *ba-ni-in-gar*.
63. H: *-da-* for *-dè-*.   64. So I; the reading in A is uncertain.   65. I adds *-e*.
66. I and J insert *-in-*.   67. I probably *im-*[*me*].   68. I omits *-ra*.   69. K omits *-in-*.   70. K omits line.   71. K omits *muš-*.   72. K; *bal-?-sag-* for *kur-*.
73. K has *sipad-ganam* for *tùr-za*.   74. K and L: *-dè-* for *-da-*.   75. Between lines 186 and 187, K and L insert two lines, thus: [*lugal*]*-zu dug₄-ga-ni nam-mu daḫ-a-ni nam-mu*; [*lugal-m*]*u a-na bi-in-dug₄* [*a-na b*]*i-in-daḫ-àm*.   76. E omits *-in-*.
77. So clearly in E, in A the sign seems to be RIN.   78. E: *bar* for *bara*.   79. E omits *-a-*.   80. C: *ba-an-pàd* for *-pàd-da*.
81. E: *-šè(?)* for *-ke₄*.   82. C and E add *-e*.
83. E omits *-ab-*.   84. E: *-ba*.   85. C probably *-bi* for *-ba*.   86. E omits *-ab-*.
87. In E the NI between *-kal-* and *-la-* is a scribal erasure.   88. E and K omit *-ka*.
89. E omits *-aba*.   90. E: *-la-* for *-gal-gal-*.
91. H: *-ke₄* for *-ra*.   92. K adds *-dùg*.
93. K: *ga(!?)-*.   94. K omits *gurun-*.
95. K omits *-a*.   96. K omits *-a-*.   97. K seems to have *mà-e-*[*me*]*-en en-šu-sikil-la-du-ma*.   98. E: *-maḫ-* for *-lugal-*; K: *-lugal-maḫ-* for *-lugal-*.   99. J, K, and L omit *-a-*.   100. In K the verb probably read [*m*]*u-ni-ib-gi₄-gi₄*; if the copy is correct, K seems to have one or more complexes between *en-aratta^{ki}-ra* and the verb.
101. J; *-^{d}inanna* for *-an-na*.   102. J omits *-ZA*.

103. J omits -ZA. 104. J omits determinative and has -*ra* for -*ka*. 105. J, N, and O: *mu-na-ni-in* for *mu-un-di-ni-ib*; J omits -*eš*. 106. J, N, and O omit -*šè*.

107. J (and probably O): *ì-gál*; N: *i-in-gál*.

108. J omits -*a*-. 109. J and N omit -*en*.

110. J: *ḫur-še-àm* for *u₄-bi-a*. 111. J inserts -*un*-. 112. J omits -*a*-. 113. J: -*a* for -*ba*. 114. J: *im*-, and K *in*- for *ì*-.

115. P: *ì*- for *in*-. 116. K: *im-da-an-gál*.

117. K: *mu-na*- for *mu-un-di*-. 118. K omits -*a*-.

119. K adds -*šè*. 120. K inserts -*ra*- before -*àm*.

121. G probably inserts the determinative *mušen* before -*na*. 122. G: -*ma* for -*ba*.

123. Note that the copy of E omits -*na*.

124. K: -*re*. 125. K has several signs following -*e₁₁*; note that the copy of E fails to indicate that there is room for MÙŠ between *kur*- and -*e₁₁*. 126. Line omitted in E and K. 127. E omits -*ba*-.

128. E omits -*a*. 129. E too perhaps -*an* in spite of copy. 130. E: -*ke*.

131. E omits -*en*; the *mu*- is certain in E, but the traces in A point to a variant.

132. E: -*me*- for -*e*-. 133. E: *dù*-.

134. E: *ḫu-mu-ši-dib*. 135. E omits *gud*-.

136. E omits -*a*-. 137. E: -*na-ni-ib*.

138. E: ....*ᵈutu é-bi-è-gim*. 139. E and J omit -*e*-. 140. E: -*ka*. 141. E and M: -*ka* for *šè*. 142. E omits -*na*-.

143. E omits -*na-an*-. 144. E omits -*an*-.

145. J: -*ma*-. 146. J: *na-àm*- for *nam*-.

147. J omits *mu*-. 148. J omits -*e*.

149. J inserts -*un*-. 150. J adds -*en*.

151. J: -*ra*. 152. J omits -*ra*- and adds -*im* in the last complex but one, and adds -*im* in the last complex. 153. J: -*a*- for -*ra*-.

154. J adds -*šè*; K seems to have a variant writing for *ešemen*, thus KI.A.NE-[ᵈINANNA].

155. J adds -*gim*. 156. J: *im*-. 157. J inserts -*un*-. 158. J: -*mu*. 159. Line omitted in J. 160. J: -*im*-. 161. J omits line. 162. J: -*ra-ra-a* for -*ri-ri*-.

163. P: -*igi*- for -*i-gi₈*-. 164. P: -*igi* for -*i-gi₈*. 165. J: -*ke₄*. 166. So J; A perhaps ᵍⁱˢ*li*- for *li*-. 167. J omits determinative and has -*bi* for -*e*.

168. J: *i-ni*- for *bi*-. 169. J: -*bar*- for -*bara*-.

170. J omits -*e*-. 171. J inserts a sign resembling GUR between -*an*- and -*aratta*ᵏⁱ-.

172. J omits -*ra*; note the scribal erasure.

173. J adds -LU. 174. J: *kisi₇*- for *kisi₆*-.

175. J inserts -*a*-. 176. J omits -*a*.

177. J omits *ì*-. 178. J: -*ka*. 179. So J; in A the sign between -*ta*- and -KÍD is not -AN-. 180. J inserts -*da*-. 181. J omits -*un*-. 182. J: *ki*- for *igi*-.

183. J: *ḫu-un-tùm*. 184. J: -*ka*.

185. J adds -LU. 186. J: -*ke₄*. 187. J omits determinative and has -*bi* for -*e*.

188. J: -*àm* for -*la*. 189. J inserts -*ni*-.

190. J omits -*an*-. 191. J omits one DÙG.

192. J omits -*ù*-. 193. So J; line is omitted in A. 194. J: -*mi*- for -*ši*-.

195. For lines 402-404, J has a variant text which reads: [*gi*]ˢ*ḫa-šu-úr nam-me* *gi*ˢ*šim(?) nam-me*, [*gi*]ˢ*erin nam-me* *gi*ˢ*za-ba-lum nam-me*, [*giš*]*su-ur-me* *na-nam* ᵍⁱˢ*taškarin na-nam*.

196. J: ᵍⁱˢSU-SUḪUR-*a*. 197. J: *tùm*.

198. J: -*lá*. 199.. J inserts -*i*- before final -*zi*. 200. J substitutes a line corresponding to line 101. 201. Q, if no miscopy is involved, has -*ka* for -*gim*.

202. The suggestion that BI is the last sign in in this line in Q (cf. *JAOS* 60:250) is therefore erroneous. 203. Q, if the copy is correct has [*geš*]*tug-gím* for *sig-ga*.

204. Q: -*ra* for -*úr*. 205. Q omits -*a*-.

206. Q probably so in spite of copy. 207. Q, according to the copy, has only one line missing at this point; perhaps, however, the original had two lines (439 and 440) missing. 208. Q: -*ma*- for -*a*-.

209. Perhaps *ù*- is to be restored before *mu*-.

210. So Q; J may have a sign between -*a* and *mu*-. 211. Q: *inim(!?)-dugud(!?)*.

212. Q (for the corrected reading of the line, cf. *JNES* 60:250) has *mu-e*- for *me*-.

213. Q: *ma-e*. 214. Q: *ḫé-bi-ib-dib-e*.

215. Q: *al*-BU-BU. 216. Following *lul-la-me-a*, Q reads *gú mu-na-ab-du₈-de-en*.

217. Q: -*gar* for -*sì*. 218. Q omits -*a*-.

219. Q: -*e* for -*re*. 220. S: -*a*; the sign preceding in S is difficult to read (perhaps E₁₁), the traces in A seem to point to a variant. 221. S: -*kam*. 222. Line omitted in S. 223. Line omitted in T.

224. In T the line ends in -[*ku*]*r-kur-ra*.

225. T: -*àm*. 226. T inserts -*in*-. 227. T inserts -*in*-. 228. So, in spite of copy of A.

229. T omits -*ar*. 230. T erroneously *dug₄-mu-na-ab*. 231. T inserts -*e*- before -*a*-.

232. T adds -*ar*. 233. T omits *i-ni*-.

234. Written presumably above the line because of an erroneous omission. 235. S omits *i*-.

236. S omits this line and the two following.

237. S reads -*kalag* for -*dag* in this and the following lines. 238. S: -*ka* for -*a-ke₄*.

239. S has *šu* after -*na* and omits *la*-. 240. S: -*ka* for -*ra*. 241. S has *šu* after -*ra* and omits *la*-. 242. S: -*bi*. 243. Between the two UG signs is probably an erased GÁ.

244. Note the inexplicable small DI sign under

the -*sig*.   245. Line accidentally omitted by the scribe and therefore written on left edge with a vertical line to indicate where it was to be inserted.

10

20

30

40

50

Ni 9601(A)

obverse col. i

60

70

80

90

100

110

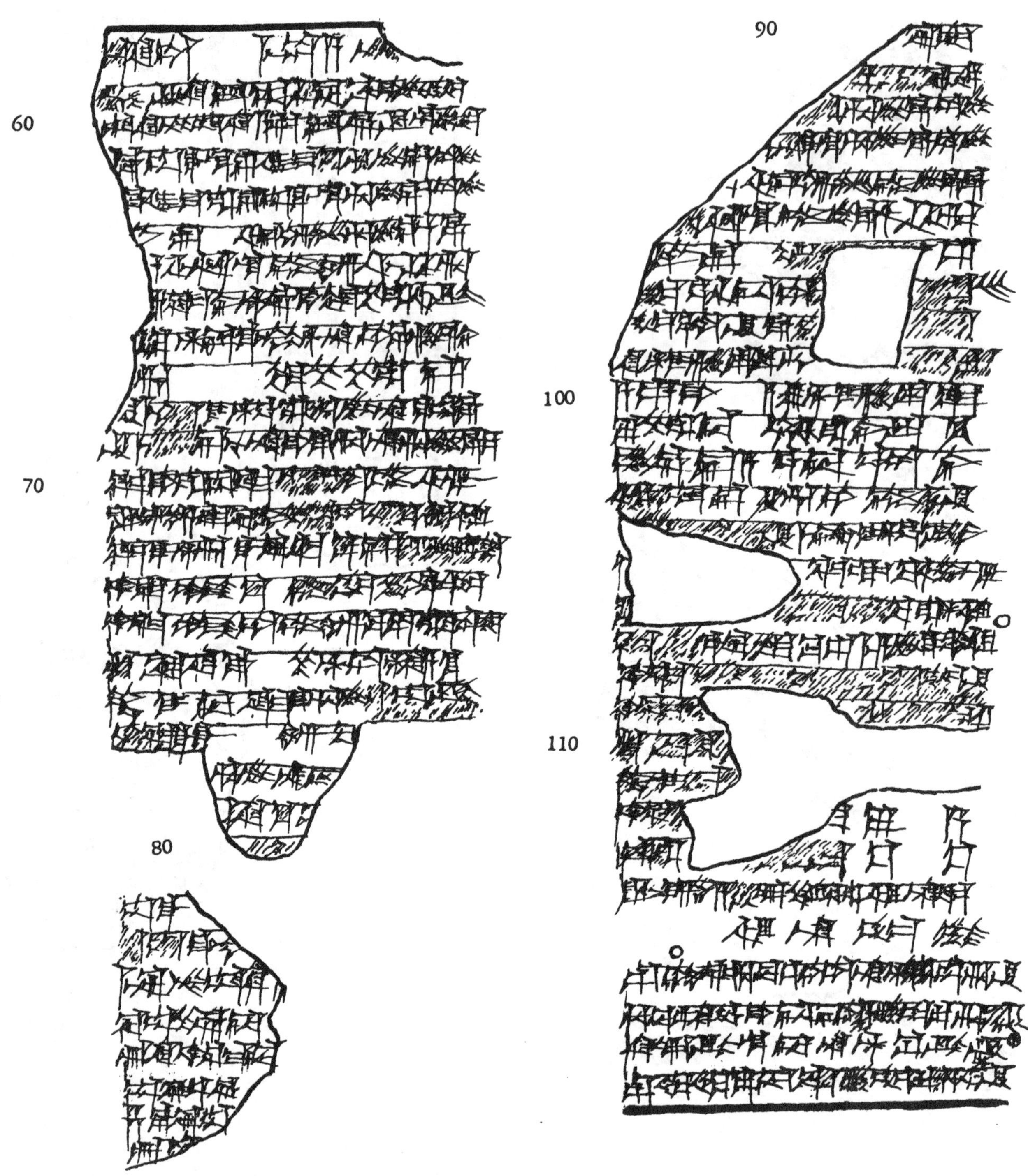

Ni 9601(A)

obverse col. ii

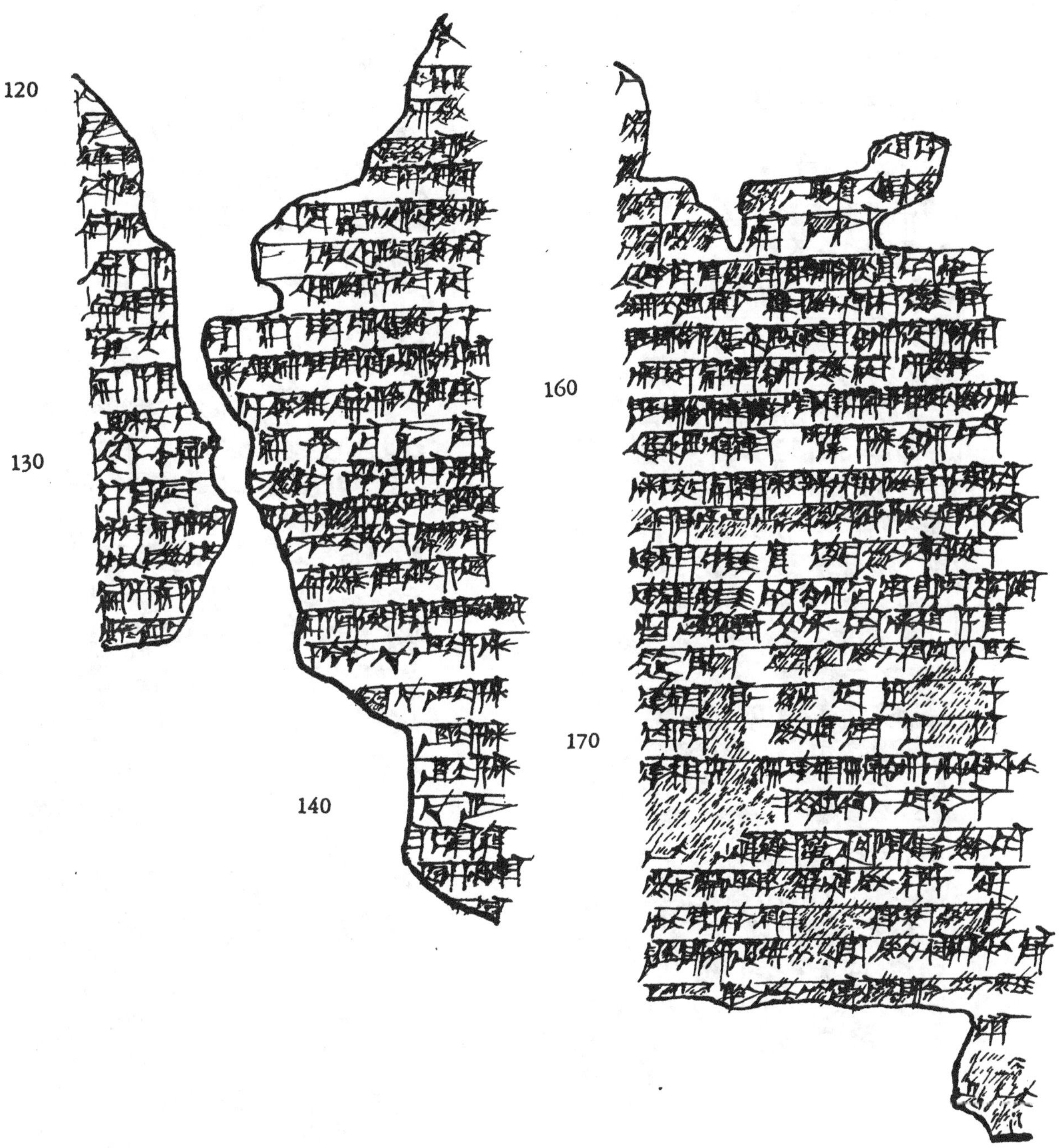

Ni 9601(A)

obverse col. iii

Ni 9601(A)

obverse col. iv

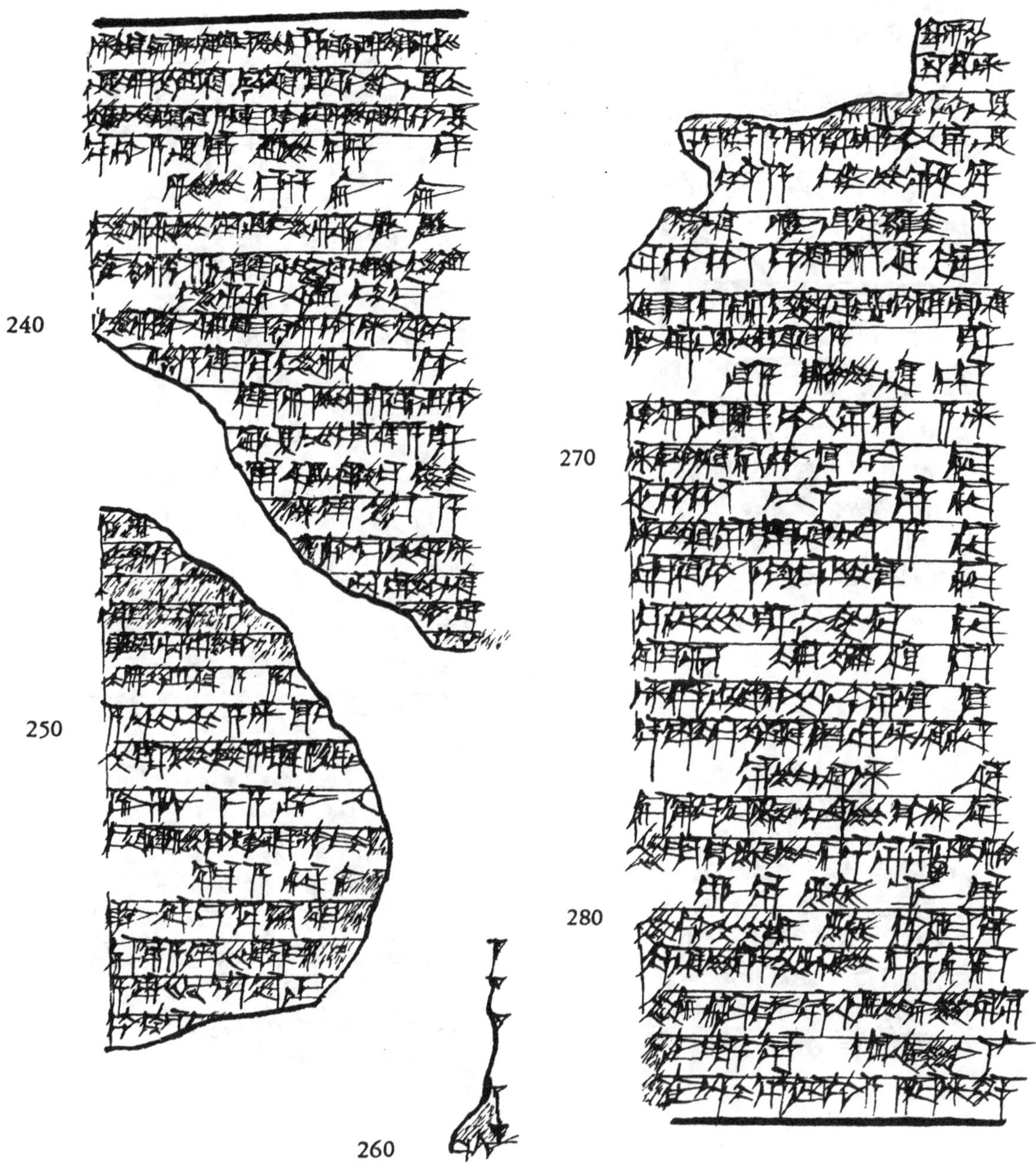

Ni 9601(A)

obverse col. v

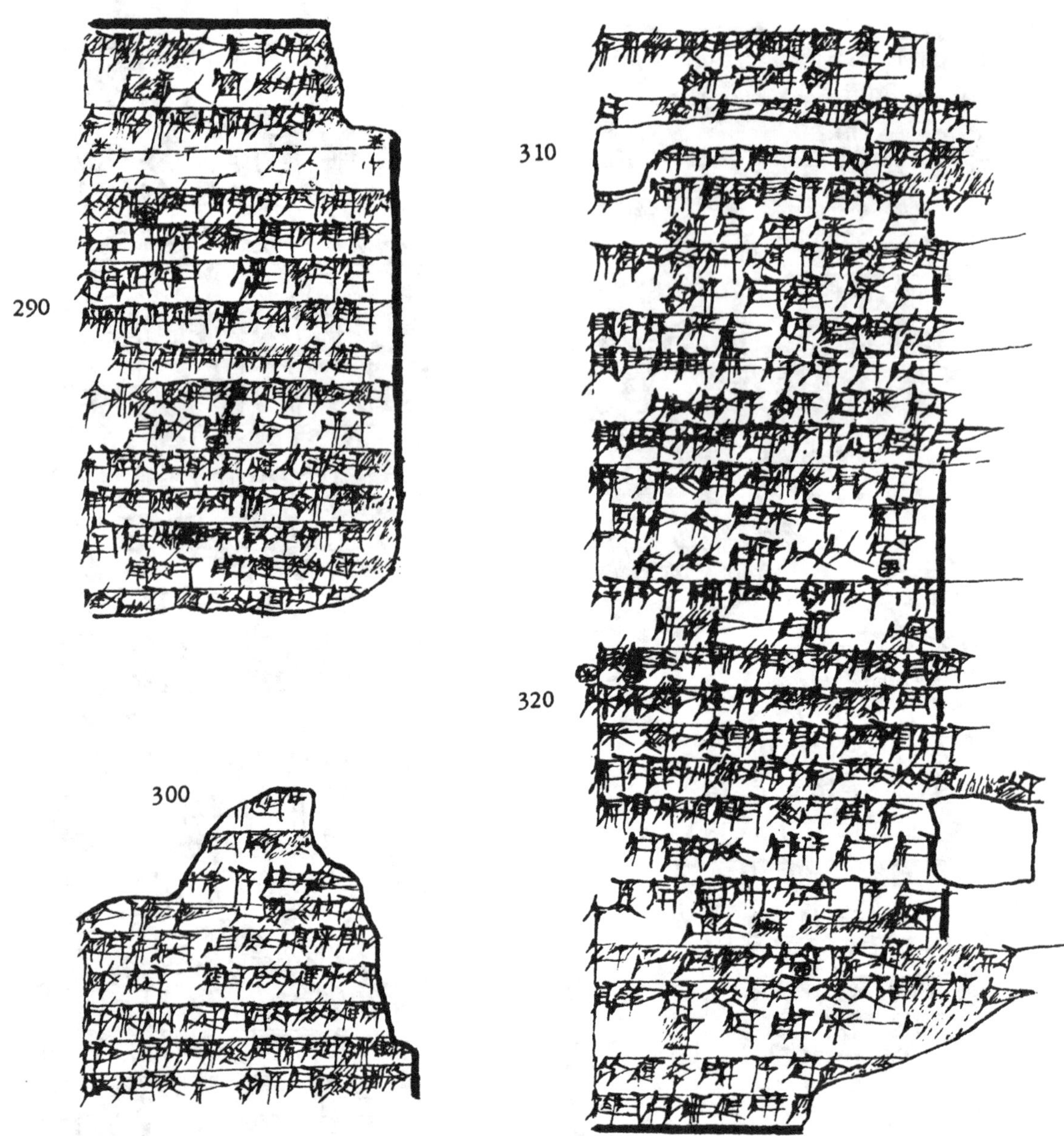

Ni 9601(A)

obverse col. vi

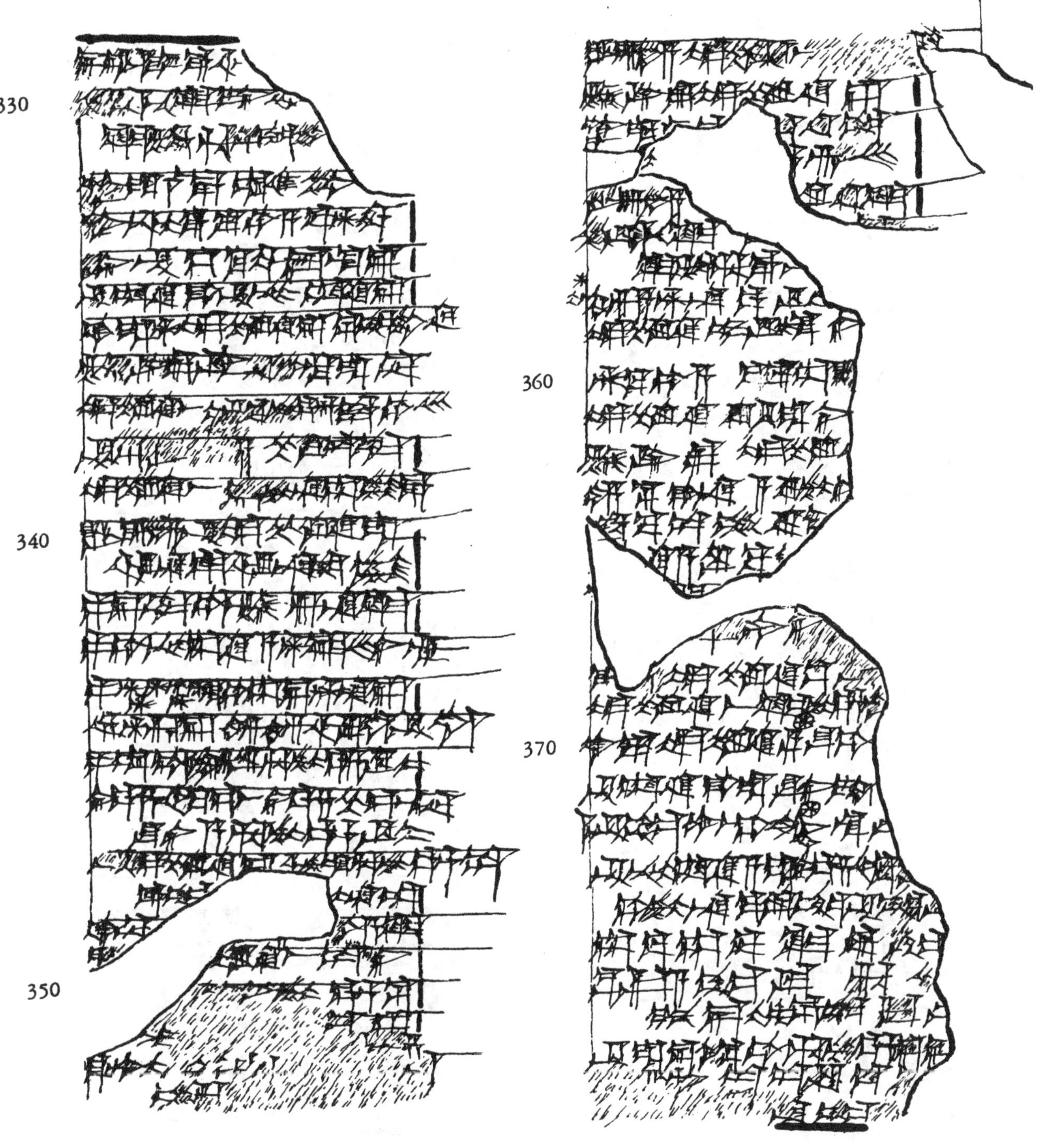

330

340

350

360

370

Ni 9601 (A)

reverse col. vii

380

390

400(!)

410

420

Ni 9601 (A)

reverse col. viii

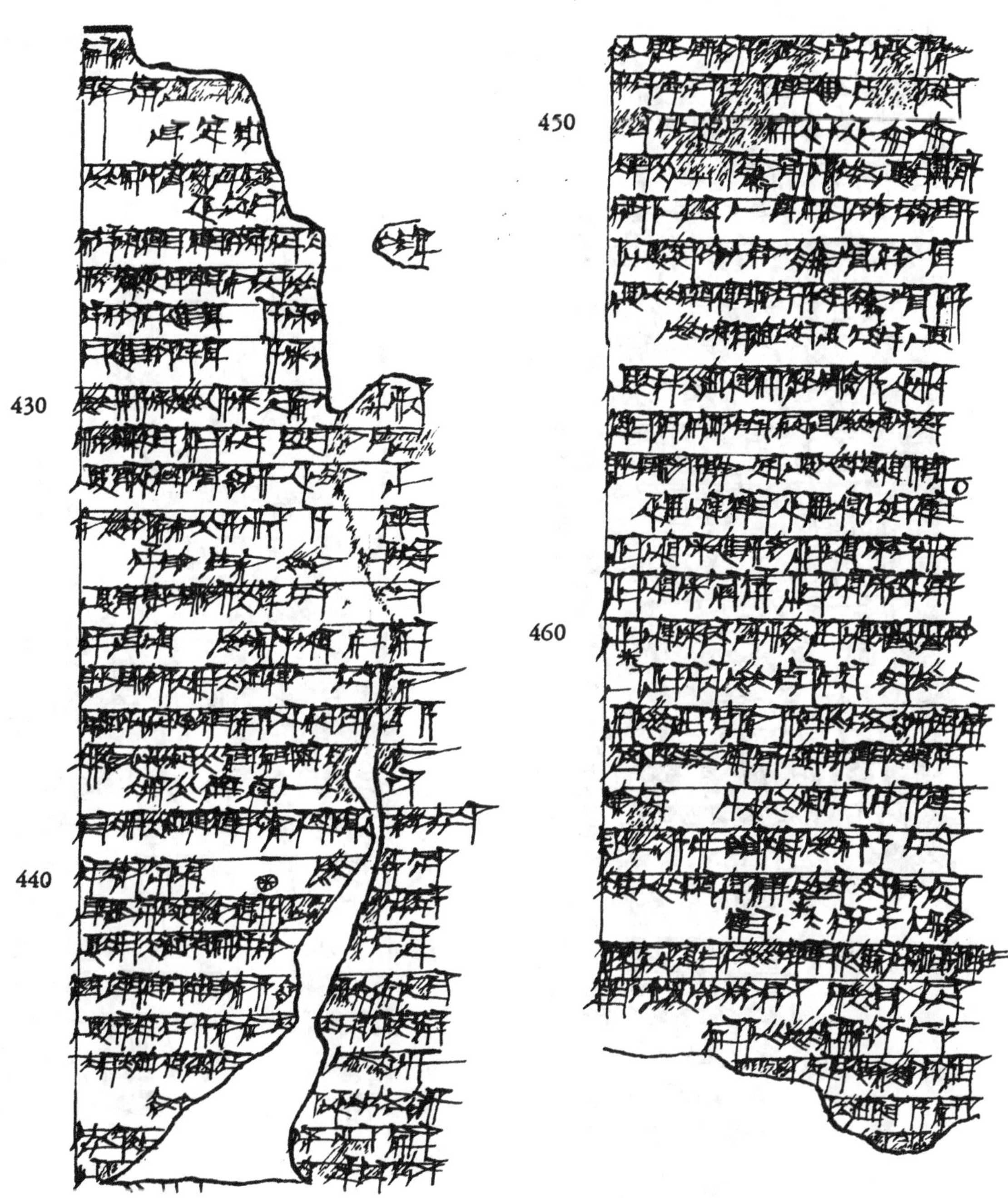

Ni 9601(A)

reverse col. ix

470
480
490
500
510
520

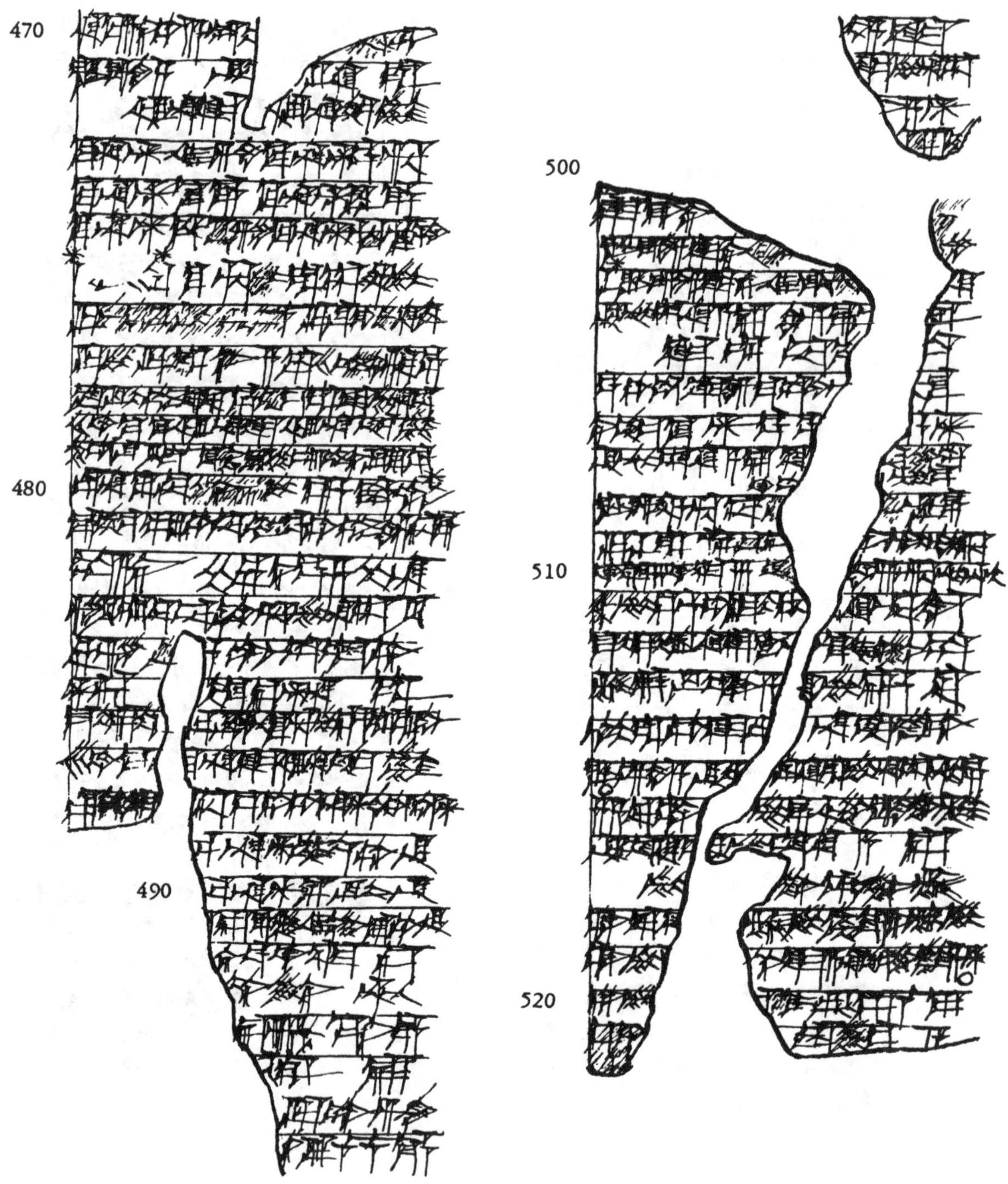

Ni 9601(A)

reverse col. x

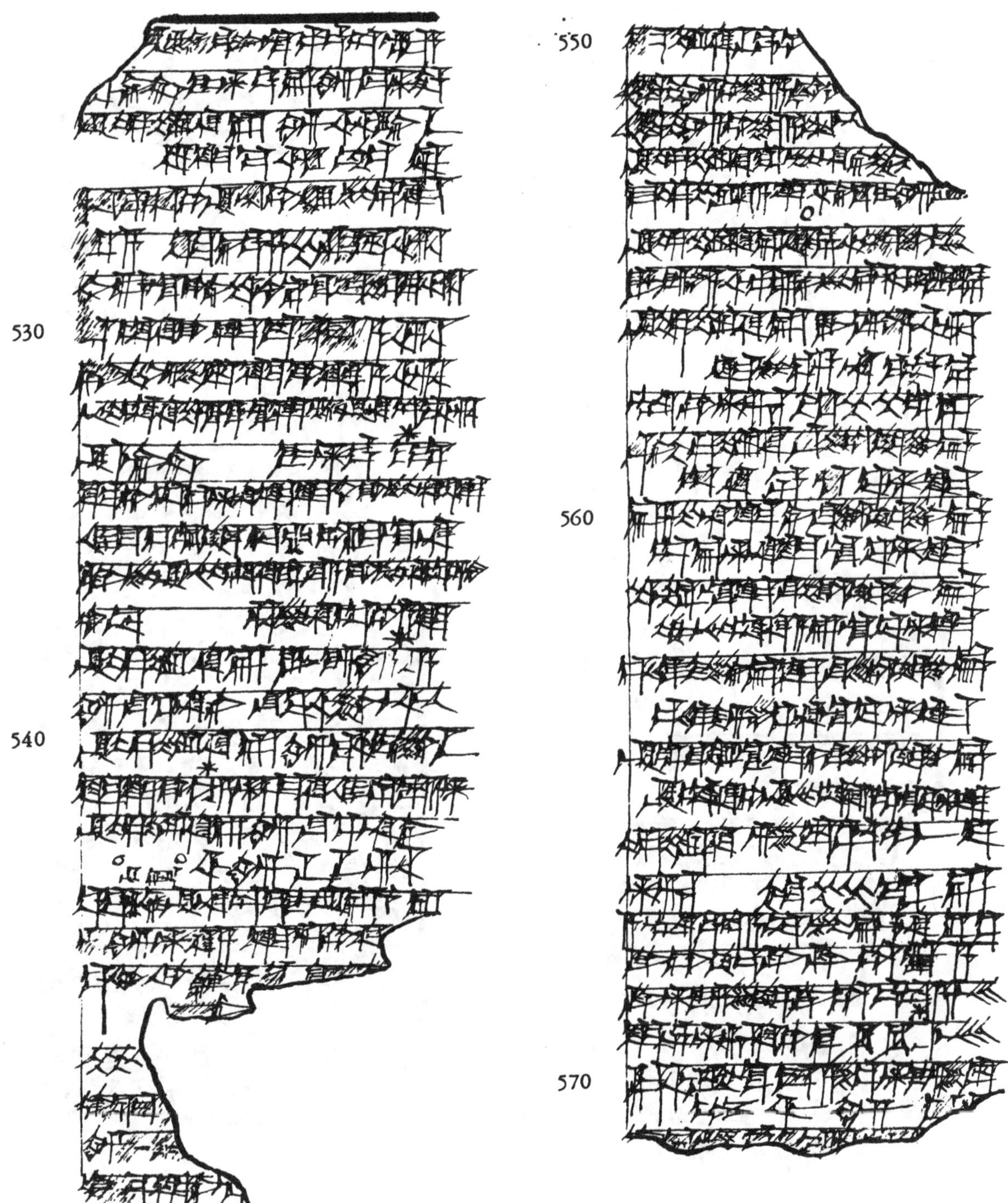

Ni 9601(A)

reverse col. xi

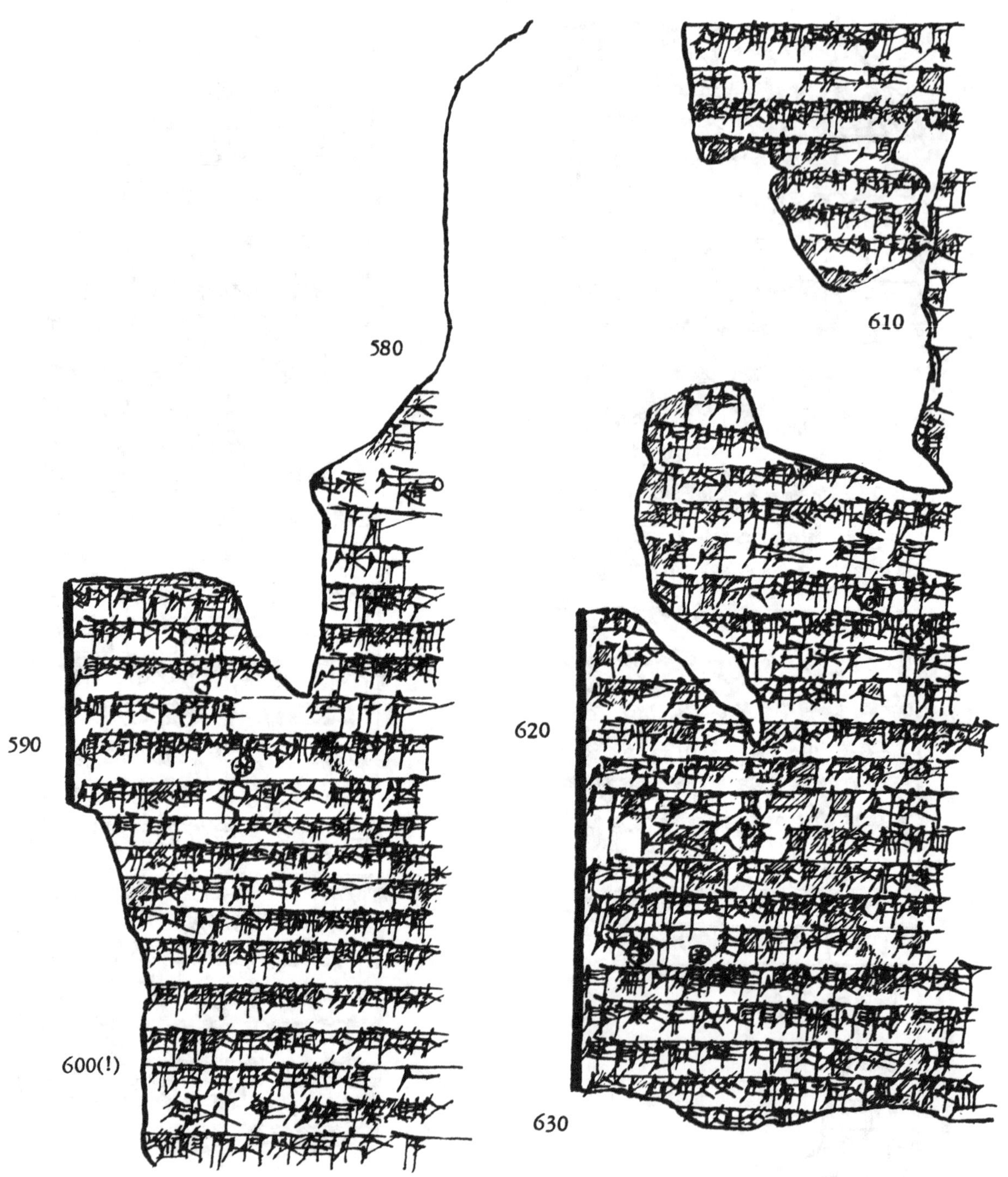

Ni 9601(A)

reverse col. xii

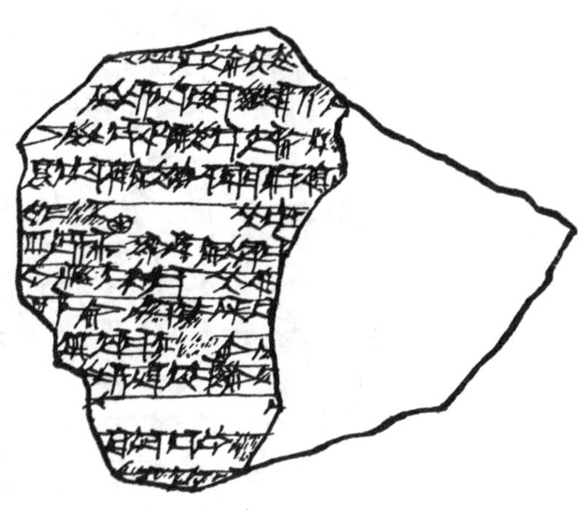

Ni 9733 (L)

reverse (obverse destroyed)

631

Ni 9601 (A)

left edge

Ni 9700 (N)

reverse (obverse destroyed)

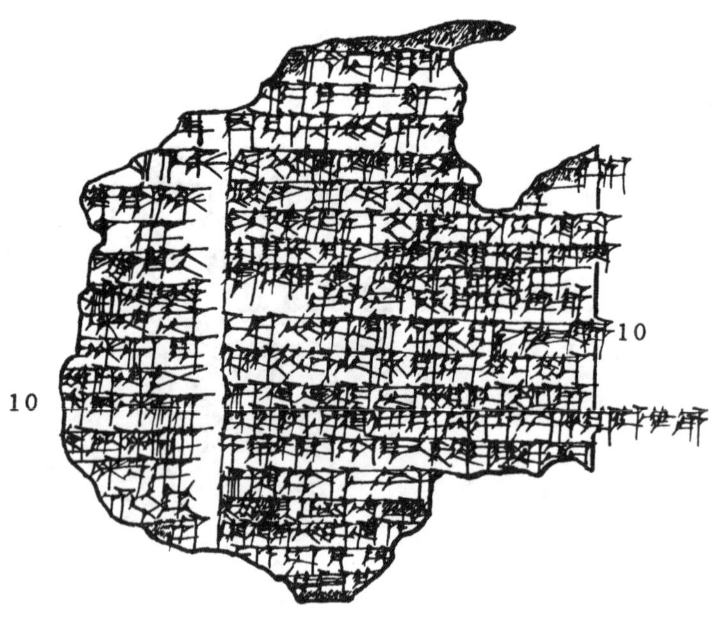

UM 29-16-422(C)

obverse

UM 29-16-422(C)

reverse

obverse

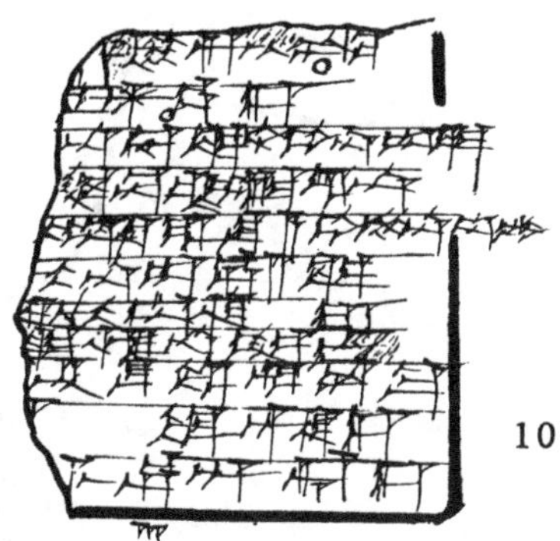

reverse

Ni 4529(H)

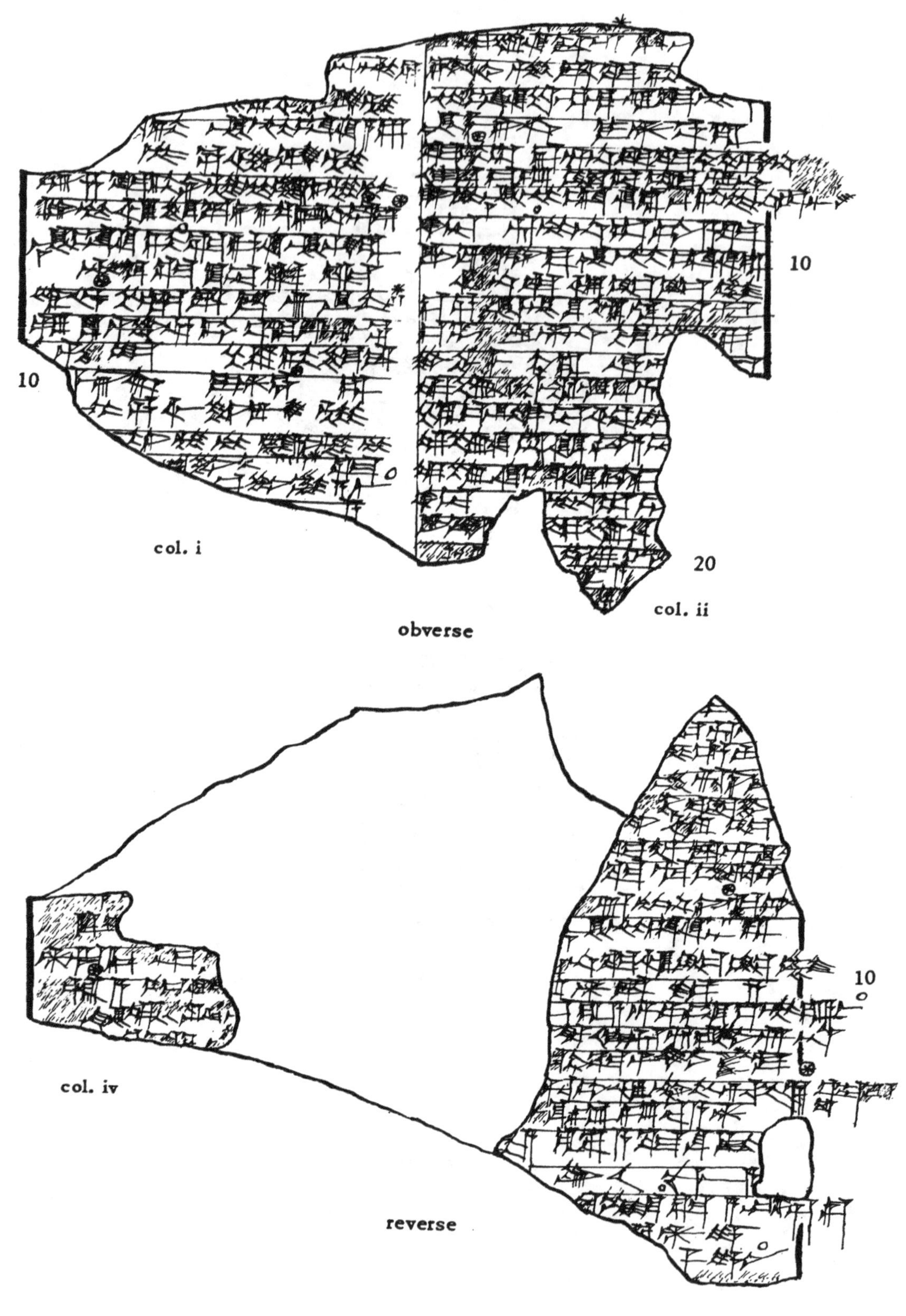

Ni 4361 + 4440(K)

Ni 9601(A)

obverse

Ni 9601(A)

reverse

obverse

reverse

UM 29-13-194 (A)

obverse

(reverse destroyed)

N 4130 (B)

Photographs by Reuben Goldberg

reverse

obverse

UM 29-16-422 (C)

Photographs by Reuben Goldberg

obverse

reverse

N 6277(D)

Photographs by Reuben Goldberg

obverse

SEM 14 (E)

Photograph by Reuben Goldberg

reverse

SEM 14 (E)

Photograph by Reuben Goldberg

obverse

reverse

PBS XIII 8 (G)

obverse

reverse

N 3236 (I)

Photographs by Reuben Goldberg

obverse

SEM 16 (J)

Photograph by Reuben Goldberg

reverse

SEM 16 (J)

Photograph by Reuben Goldberg

obverse   reverse

HGT 8 (P)

reverse

(obverse destroyed)

N 3623 (R)

Photographs by Reuben Goldberg

reverse (obverse destroyed)

N 3623 (O)

obverse

reverse

CBS 2291 (T)

Photographs by Reuben Goldberg